THE KINDERGARTEN
BIG GET READY
BOOK

AUTHORS
BARBARA GREGORICH
MARTHA PALMER

ILLUSTRATORS
RICHARD PAPE
DAVID BECKES
SHIRLEY BECKES
JOYCE JOHN
TERRI HUIZINGA
JANE CONTEH-MORGEN

The Kindergarten **Big Get Ready** Book is a compilation of favorite titles from the **Get Ready** and **I Know It!** series. The ten titles are listed in the table of contents.

CONTENTS

PARENT GUIDE

The activities in the **Big Get Ready Book** for Kindergarten are those most commonly taught at the kindergarten level. Here are some suggestions for working with your child at home:

- Don't do too many pages at one sitting. The size of the book could overwhelm the child. Remove a few pages at a time. (Pages are perforated for easy removal.) Praise each completed page. Page by page, day to day, is the best.

- If your child is puzzled by one activity, move on to another. The activities are ordered, but there's nothing magical about that order.

- Do the activities at a particular time of day, perhaps before snack time. Do them when the child is not tired. Discuss the learning experience, be enthusiastic. "Let's work in our school books today! Do you remember what you did yesterday?"

- Enjoy it! Laugh a lot! Discuss the activity. Most activities can be done independently by the child since directions are clear and consistent. Never use an activity as punishment. Don't expect too much. The activities are meant as practice.

- There will be days when your child may not feel like working. This is typical, so accept it. And remember: the communication patterns you establish today will pay off as your child grows older.

How high can you count?

1 2 3 4 5 6 7 8 9 10 11 12

12

11 12

10 11 12

9 10 11 12

8 9 10 11 12

7 8 9 10 11 12

6 7 8 9 10 11 12

5 6 7 8 9 10 11 12

4 5 6 7 8 9 10 11 12

3 4 5 6 7 8 9 10 11 12

2 3 4 5 6 7 8 9 10 11 12

1 2 3 4 5 6 7 8 9 10 11 12

1
one

Trace 1. Then write 1.

| |

Trace one. Then write one.

one

Circle everything that there is only one of below.

2
two

Trace 2. Then write 2.

2

Trace two. Then write two.

two

Circle all the things that there are two of below.

7

3
three

Trace 3. Then write 3.

3 - - - - - - - - - - - - - - - -

Trace three. Then write three.

three - - - - - - - - - - - -

Circle all the things that there are three of below.

9

4
four

Trace 4. Then write 4.

4 -

Trace four. Then write four.

four -

Circle all the things that there are four of below.

11

5
five

Trace 5. Then write 5.

5 - - - - - - - - - -

Trace five. Then write five.

five - - - - - - - -

Circle all the things that there are five of below.

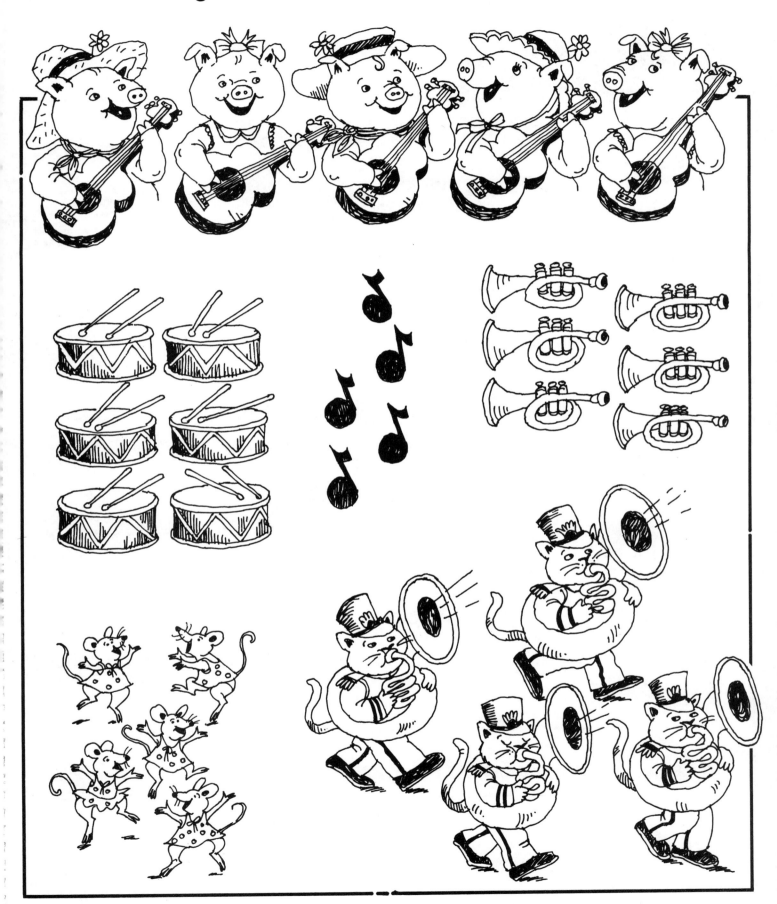

6
six

Trace 6. Then write 6.

6

Trace six. Then write six.

six

Circle all the things that there are six of below.

7
seven

Trace 7. Then write 7.

7 ------------------------------

Trace seven. Then write seven.

seven

Circle all the things that there are seven of below.

8
eight

Trace 8. Then write 8.

8

Trace eight. Then write eight.

eight

18

Circle all the things that there are eight of below.

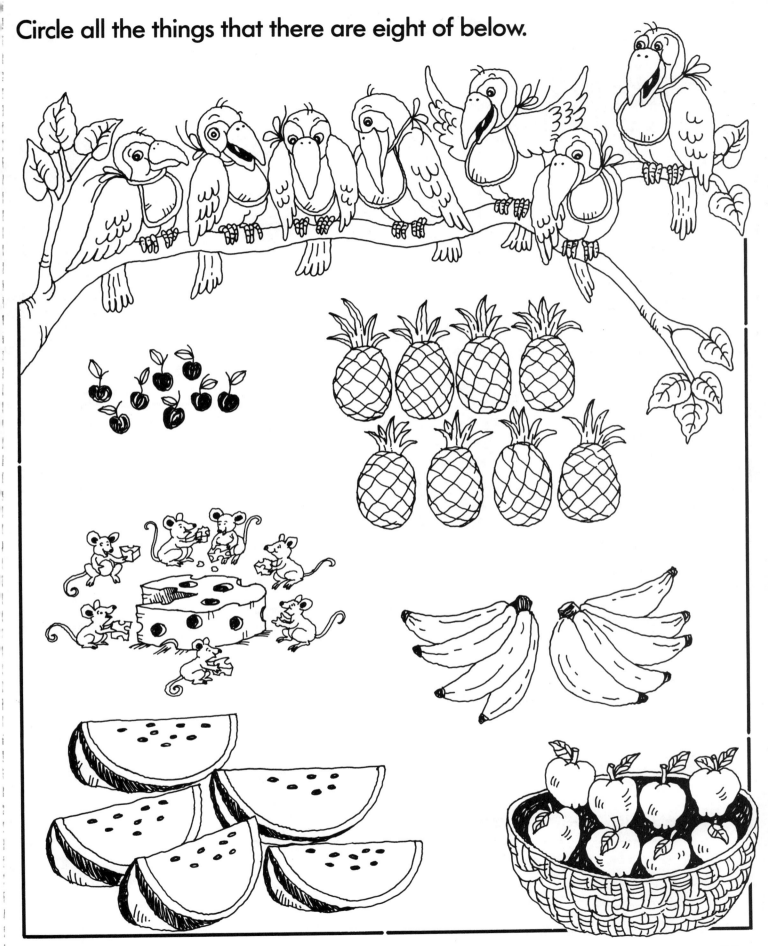

9
nine

Trace 9. Then write 9.

9

Trace nine. Then write nine.

nine

20

Circle all the things that there are nine of below.

10
ten

Trace 10. Then write 10.

10

Trace ten. Then write ten.

ten

22

Circle all the things that there are ten of below.

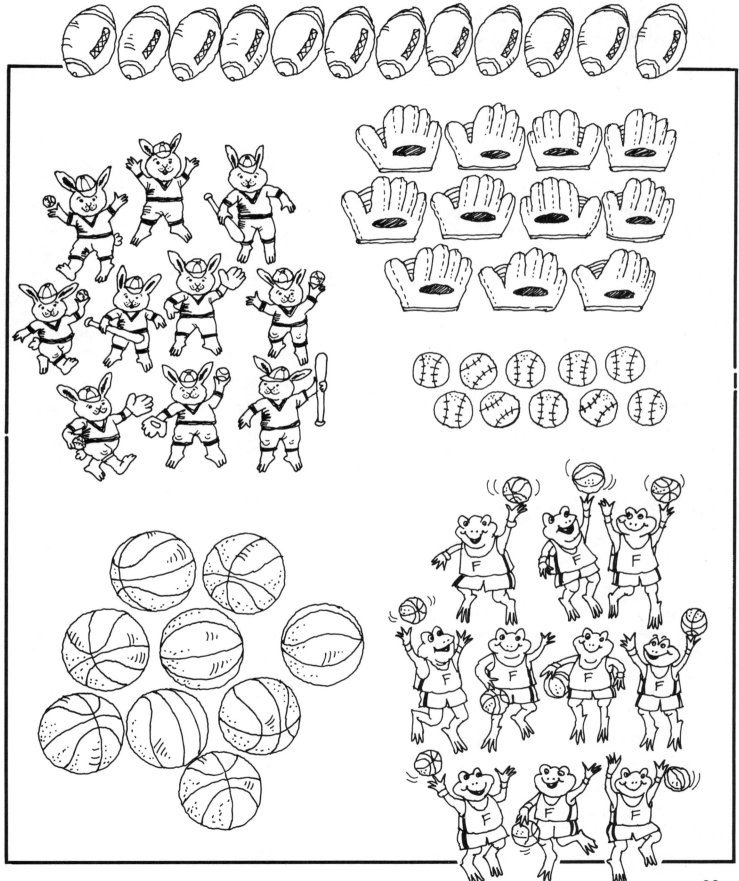

11
eleven

Trace 11. Then write 11.

11

Trace eleven. Then write eleven.

eleven

Circle all the things that there are eleven of below.

12
twelve

Trace 12. Then write 12.

12 - - - - - - - - - - - - - - - -

Trace twelve. Then write twelve.

twelve - - - - - - - - - - - - - -

Circle all the things that there are twelve of below.

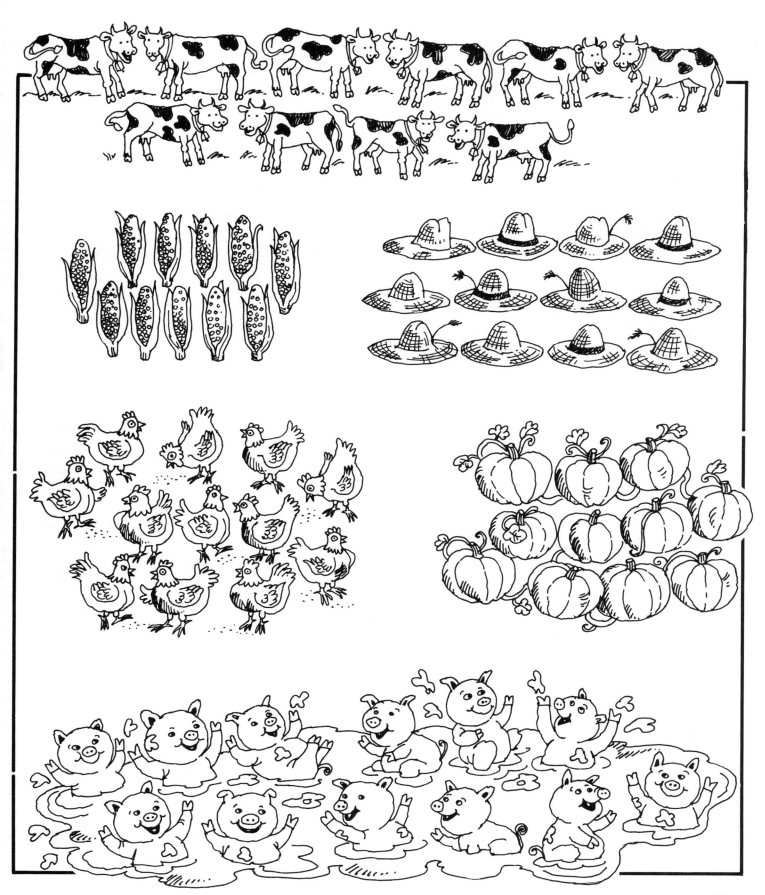

Write the correct number on each line.

How many  ? _ _ _ _ _ _ _ _

How many  ? _ _ _ _ _ _ _ _

How many  ? _ _ _ _ _ _ _ _

Circle the number that is the same as the word.

three   6   7   3   2

six   6   8   4   1

eleven   12   7   3   11

five   10   5   2   4

Draw a line from each set of sheep to the correct pen.

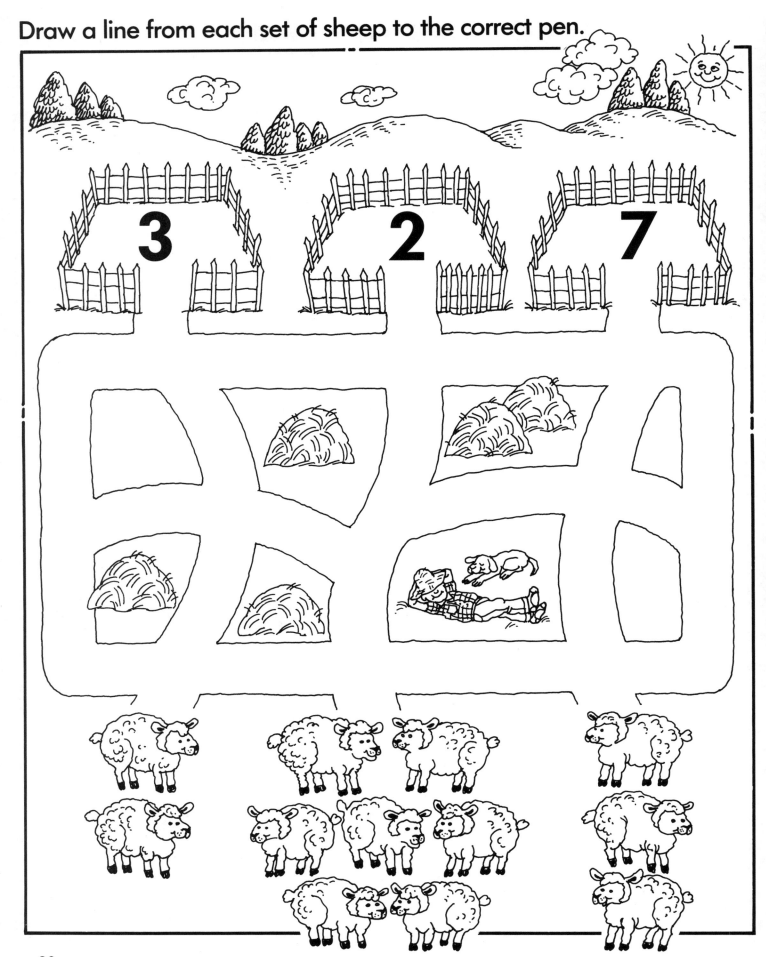

Write the correct number on each line.

How many  ? _ _ _ _ _ _ _

How many  ? _ _ _ _ _ _ _

How many  ? _ _ _ _ _ _ _

Circle the number that is the same as the word.

four   4   3   5   10

twelve   7   10   12   1

nine   5   9   6   8

two   1   12   2   4

Aa

These pictures begin with the A sound. Color them.

Trace each letter. Then write each letter.

A

a

Circle the picture that begins with the A sound.

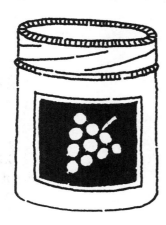 

Bb

These pictures begin with the B sound. Color them.

Trace each letter. Then write each letter.

B

b

Circle the picture that begins with the B sound.

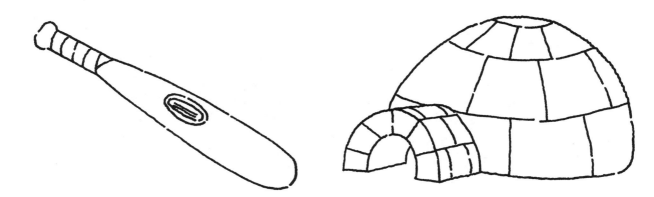

34

Cc

These pictures begin with the C sound. Color them.

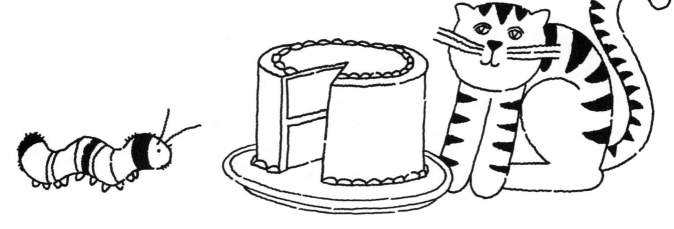

Trace each letter. Then write each letter.

C -

c -

Circle the picture that begins with the C sound.

Dd

These pictures begin with the D sound. Color them.

Trace each letter. Then write each letter.

D

d

Circle the picture that begins with the D sound.

E e

Trace each letter. Then write each letter.

E

e

Circle the picture that begins with the E sound.

Ff

These pictures begin with the F sound. Color them.

Trace each letter. Then write each letter.

F -

f -

Circle the picture that begins with the F sound.

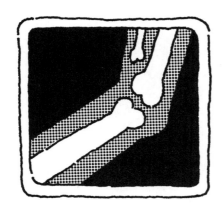

38

Gg

These pictures begin with the G sound. Color them.

Trace each letter. Then write each letter.

G

g

Circle the picture that begins with the G sound.

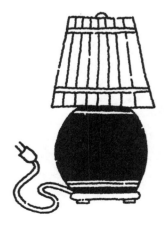

Hh

These pictures begin with the H sound. Color them.

Trace each letter. Then write each letter.

H

h

Circle the picture that begins with the H sound.

40

Ii

These pictures begin with the I sound. Color them.

Trace each letter. Then write each letter.

I

i

Circle the picture that begins with the I sound.

Jj

These pictures begin with the J sound. Color them.

Trace each letter. Then write each letter.

J

j

Circle the picture that begins with the J sound.

Kk

These pictures begin with the K sound. Color them.

Trace each letter. Then write each letter.

K ----------------------------------

k ----------------------------------

Circle the picture that begins with the K sound.

Ll

These pictures begin with the L sound. Color them.

Trace each letter. Then write each letter.

Circle the picture that begins with the L sound.

Mm

These pictures begin with the **M** sound. Color them.

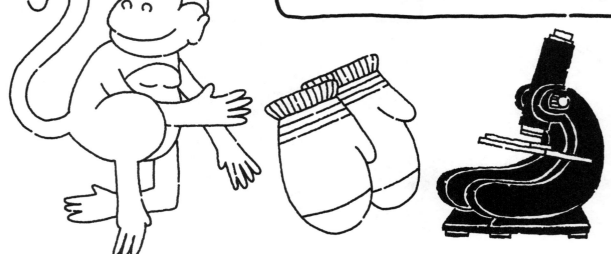

Trace each letter. Then write each letter.

M -

m -

Circle the picture that begins with the **M** sound.

N n

These pictures begin with the N sound. Color them.

Trace each letter. Then write each letter.

N

n

Circle the picture that begins with the N sound.

46

O o

These pictures begin with the O sound. Color them.

Trace each letter. Then write each letter.

Circle the picture that begins with the O sound.

P p

These pictures begin with the P sound. Color them.

Trace each letter. Then write each letter.

P

P

Circle the picture that begins with the P sound.

Q q

These pictures begin with the Q sound. Color them.

Trace each letter. Then write each letter.

Q

q

Circle the picture that begins with the Q sound.

Rr

These pictures begin with the R sound. Color them.

Trace each letter. Then write each letter.

R

r

Circle the picture that begins with the R sound.

50

Ss

Trace each letter. Then write each letter.

S

s

Circle the picture that begins with the S sound.

T t

These pictures begin with the T sound. Color them.

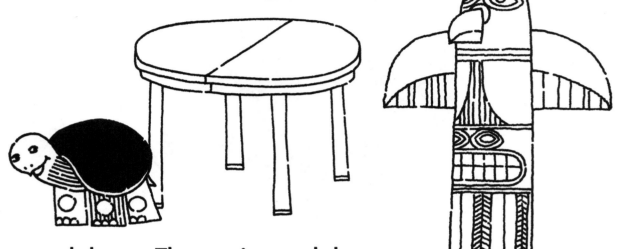

Trace each letter. Then write each letter.

Circle the picture that begins with the T sound.

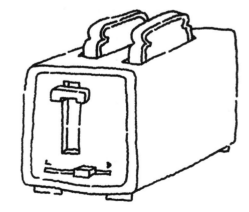

52

U u

This picture begins with the U sound. Color it.

Trace each letter. Then write each letter.

U

u

Circle the picture that begins with the U sound.

V v

These pictures begin with the V sound. Color them.

Trace each letter. Then write each letter.

V _ _ _ _ _ _ _ _ _ _ _ _

V _ _ _ _ _ _ _ _ _ _ _ _

Circle the picture that begins with the V sound.

54

W w

These pictures begin with the W sound. Color them.

Trace each letter. Then write each letter.

W

w

Circle the picture that begins with the W sound.

This picture begins with the X sound. Color it.

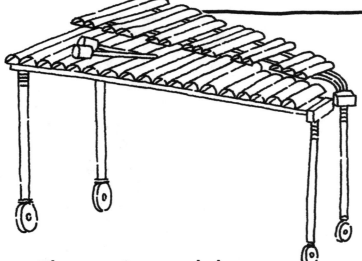

Trace each letter. Then write each letter.

X

x

Circle the picture that begins with the X sound.

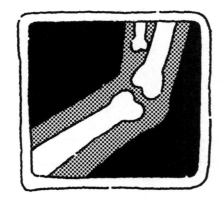

Yy

These pictures begin with the Y sound. Color them.

Trace each letter. Then write each letter.

Y

y

Circle the picture that begins with the Y sound.

57

Zz

These pictures begin with the Z sound. Color them.

Trace each letter. Then write each letter.

Z -

z -

Circle the picture that begins with the Z sound.

Write the letter that each picture begins with.

Write the letter that each picture begins with.

Write the letter that each picture begins with.

Write the letter that each picture begins with.

Write the letter that each picture begins with.

A Rhonda Rhinoceros
Award

This is to certify that

name:

_____

- -

_____

has completed the School Zone ALPHABET workbook.

Rhonda Rhinoceros

I KNOW IT!

Circle the hidden ⚔ and 📦.

Circle the hidden  and  .

Circle the hidden  and .

Circle the hidden , , and .

Circle the hidden 🐢, ⌚, and 👓.

Circle the hidden ⚊, ⚊, and ⚊.

Circle the hidden  , , and .

Circle the hidden , ⋈, 🎩, and 🔦.

Circle the hidden  **,** **,**  **, and** .

Circle the **5** hidden  .

Circle the **5** hidden ⌒.

Circle the **5** hidden .

Circle the **6** hidden .

Circle the **6** hidden ⟶

Circle the **6** hidden .

Circle the **10** hidden .

Color the **2** .

Color the **2** .

Color the **2** 🎺.

Color the **3** .

Color the **3** .

Color the **3** ⬭.

Color the 4 .

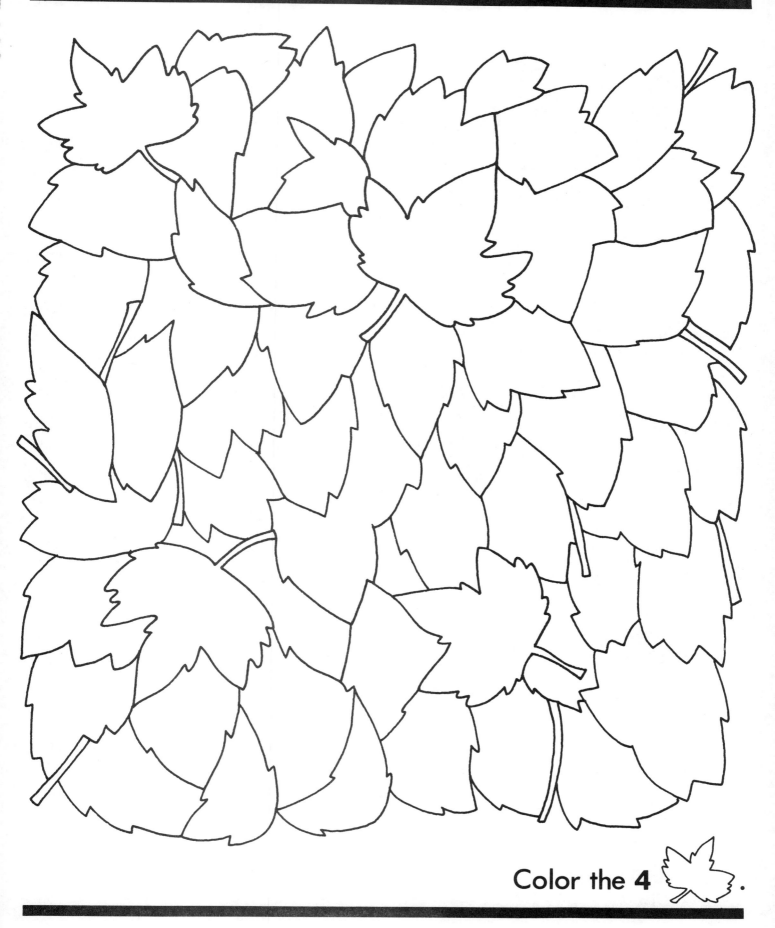

Color the **4** .

Color the **5** .

Color the **5** ⬭.

Circle the letter **C**.   Circle the letter **E**.   Circle the letter **O**.

Circle the letter **J**.   Circle the letter **L**.   Circle the letter **Z**.

Circle the letter **H**.   Circle the letter **T**.   Circle the letter **U**.

94

Circle the letter **M**.   Circle the letter **Q**.   Circle the letter **R**.

Circle the letter **B**.   Circle the letter **S**.   Circle the letter **Y**.

Circle the picture that **belongs** with the first one.

Circle the picture that **belongs** with the first one.

Circle the picture that **belongs** with the first one.

Circle the picture that **belongs** with the first one.

Circle the picture that **belongs** with the first one.

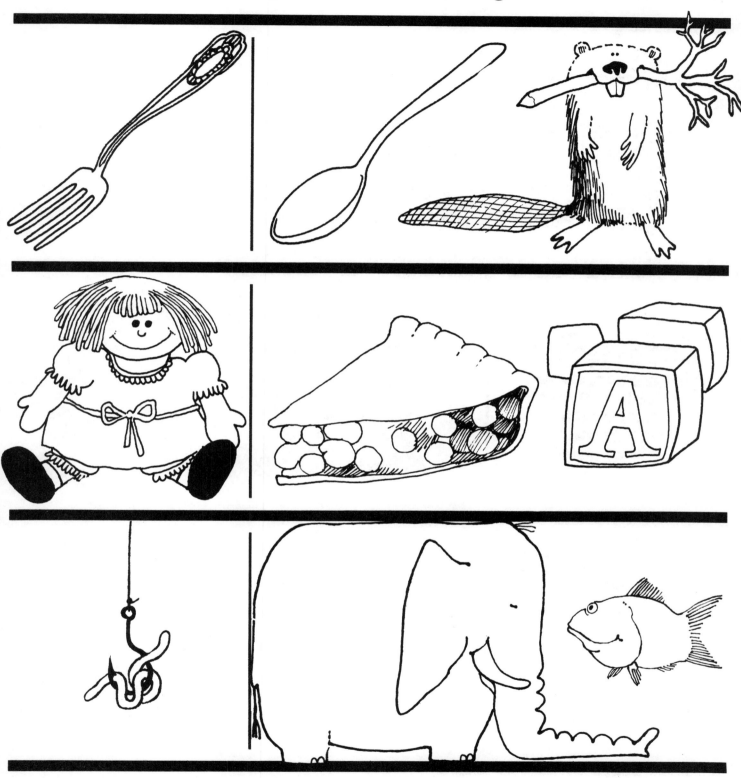

Circle the picture that **belongs** with the first one.

Circle the picture that **belongs** with the first one to make a **pair**.

Circle the picture that **belongs** with the first one to make a **pair**.

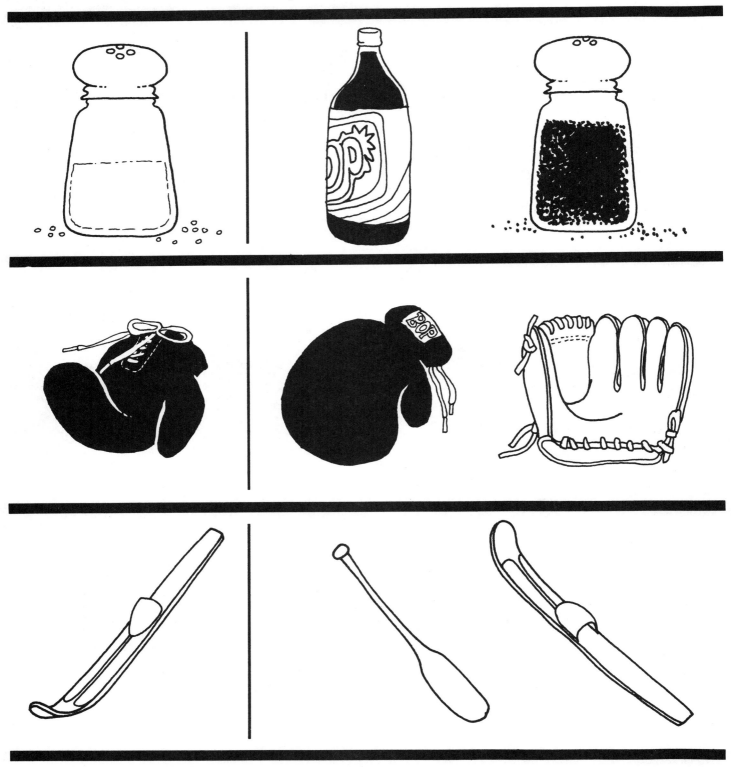

Circle the picture that **belongs** with
the first one to make a **pair**.

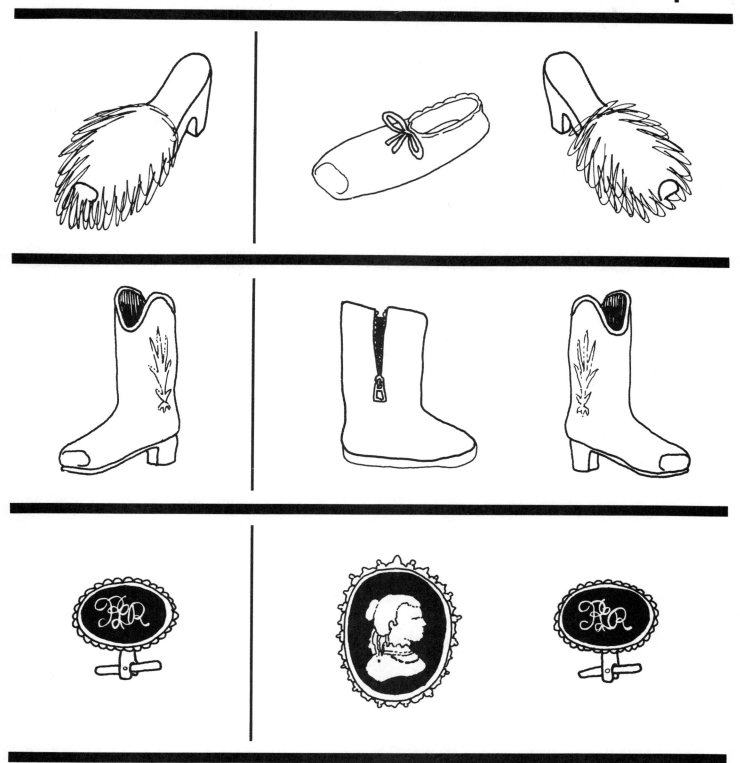

Circle the picture that **belongs** with the first one to make a **pair**.

© School Zone Publishing Company

Circle **3** things that **belong** in the ice cream store.

Circle **3** things that **belong** in the school.

Circle **3** things that **belong** in the zoo.

Circle **3** things that **belong** at the beach.

Circle the **2** pictures that **belong** with the big one.

111

Circle the **2** pictures that **belong** with the big one.

Circle the **2** pictures that **belong** with the big one.

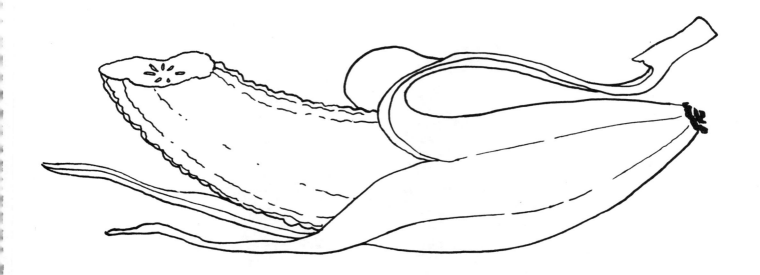

Circle the **2** pictures that **belong** with the big one.

Circle the **2** pictures that **belong** with the big one.

Circle the **2** pictures that **belong** with the big one.

Look at each group of pictures.

Circle the picture that does **not belong** in each group.

Look at each group of pictures.

Circle the picture that does **not belong** in each group.

118

Look at each group of pictures.

Circle the picture that does **not belong** in each group.

Look at each group of pictures.

Circle the picture that does **not belong** in each group.

Look at each group of pictures.

Circle the picture that does **not belong** in each group.

Look at each group of pictures.

Circle the picture that does **not belong** in each group.

Circle what does **not belong** in the picture.

Circle what does **not belong** in the picture.

Circle what does **not belong** in the picture.

Circle what does **not belong** in the picture.

Circle what does **not belong** in the picture.

Circle what does **not belong** in the picture.

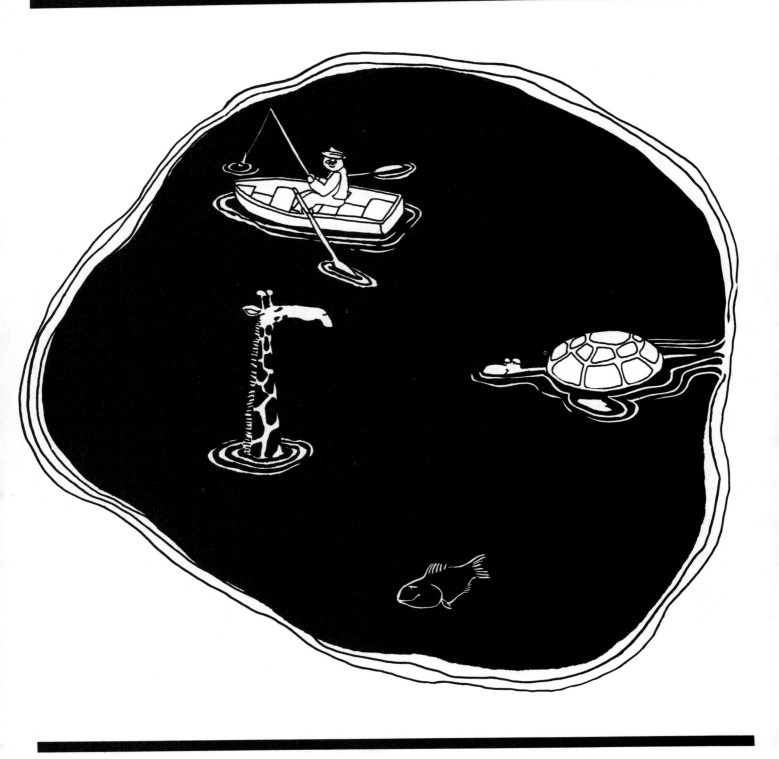

Look at each row of pictures.

Circle the picture that has something missing.

Look at each row of pictures.

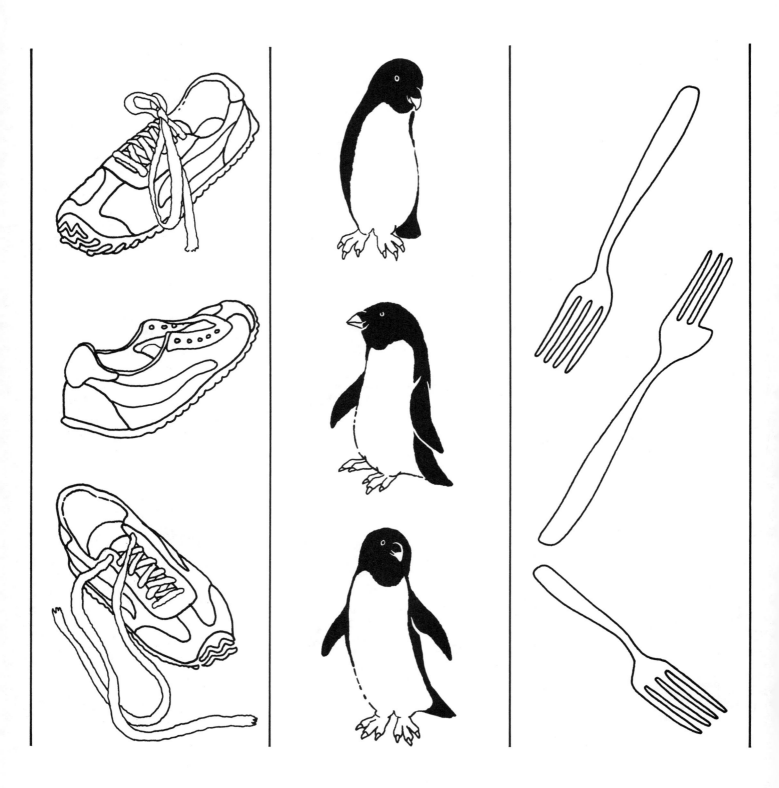

Circle the picture that has something **missing**.

Look at each row of pictures.

Circle the picture that has something **missing**.

Look at each row of pictures.

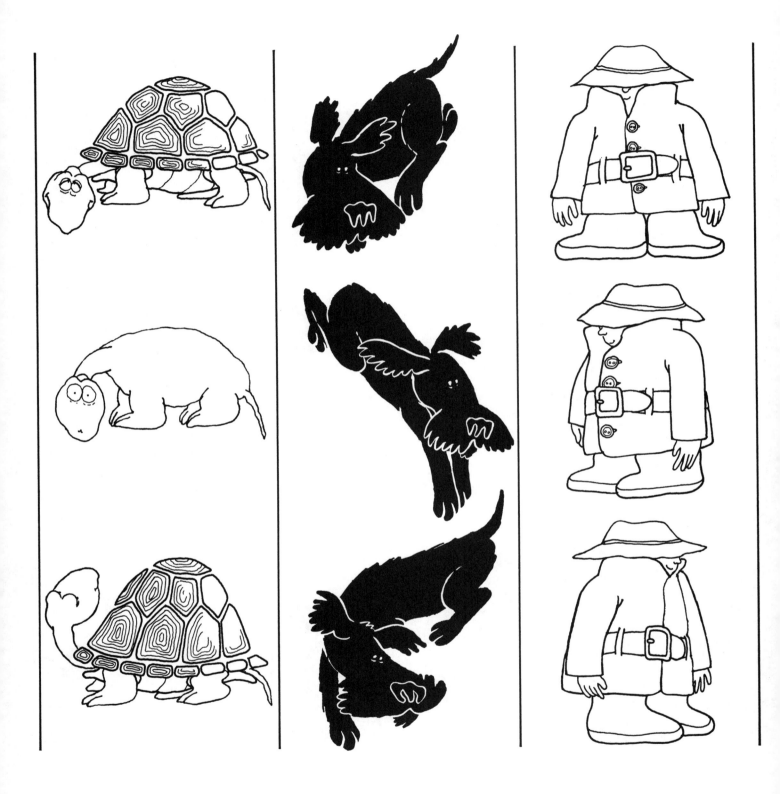

Circle the picture that has something **missing.**

Circle the part that is **missing** from the picture.

Then draw the **missing** part in the picture.

Circle the part that is **missing** from the picture.

Then draw the missing part in the picture.

Circle the part that is **missing** from the picture.

Then draw the **missing** part in the picture.

Circle the part that is **missing** from the picture.

Then draw the **missing** part in the picture.

Circle the part that is **missing** from the picture.

Then draw the **missing** part in the picture.

Circle the part that is **missing** from the picture.

Then draw the **missing** part in the picture.

Circle the part that is **missing** from the picture.

Then draw the **missing** part in the picture.

Circle the part that is **missing** from the picture.

Then draw the **missing** part in the picture.

Circle the part that is **missing** from the picture.

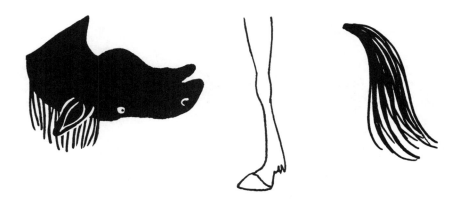

Then draw the **missing** part in the picture.

Circle the part that is **missing** from the picture.

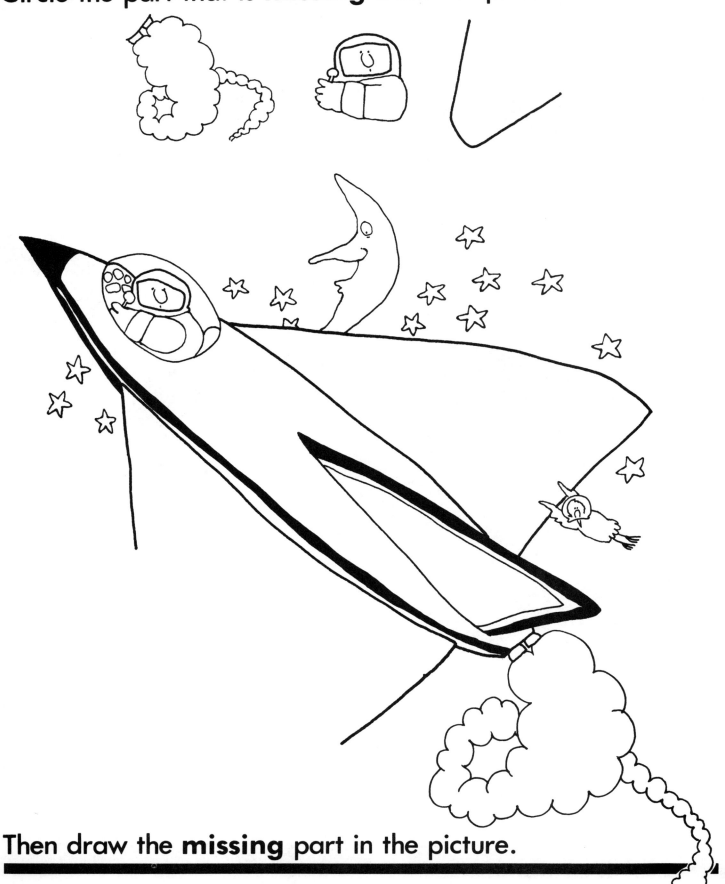

Then draw the missing part in the picture.

Circle the part that is **missing** from the picture.

Then draw the **missing** part in the picture.

Circle the part that is **missing** from the picture.

Then draw the missing part in the picture.

Circle the part that is **missing** from the picture.

Then draw the **missing** part in the picture.

Circle the part that is **missing** from the picture.

Then draw the missing part in the picture.

Circle the part that is **missing** from the picture.

Then draw the **missing** part in the picture.

Circle the part that is missing from the picture.

Then draw the missing part in the picture.

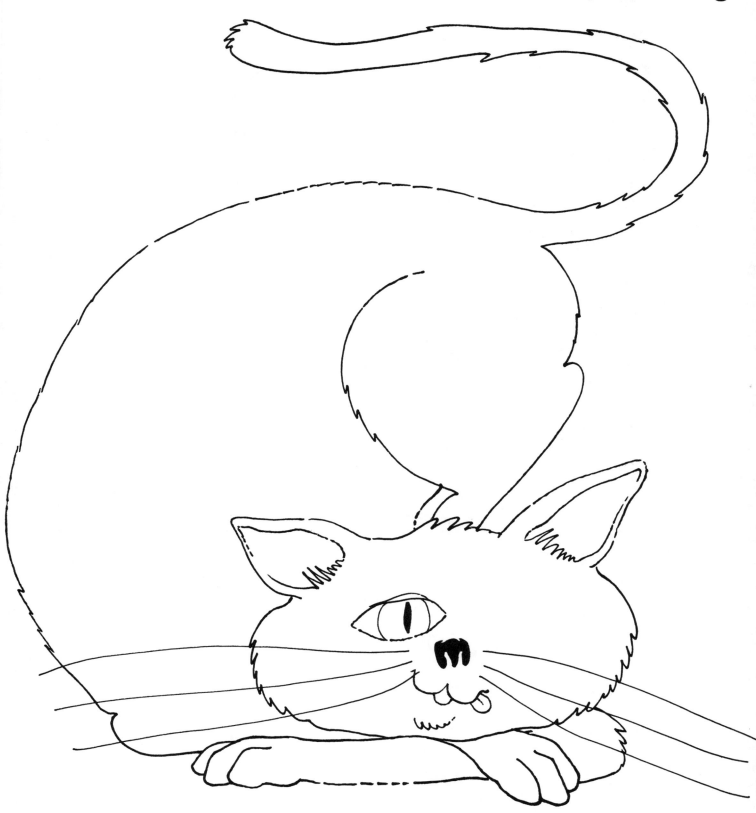

Draw the missing part in the picture.

Something is **missing!**

Draw the missing part in the picture.

Something is **missing!**

Draw the **missing** part in the picture.

Something is **missing!**

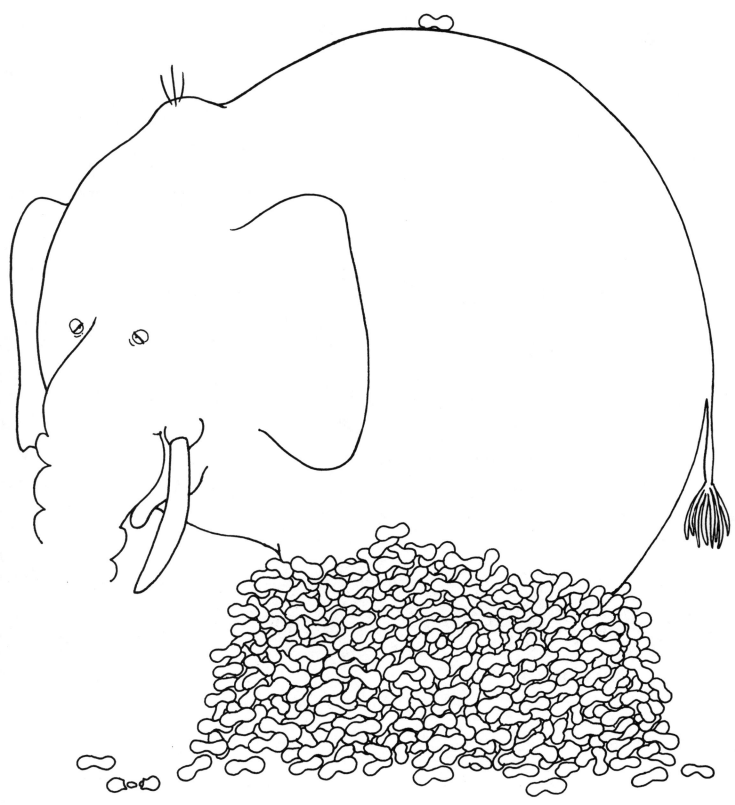

Draw the missing part in the picture.

Draw the **missing** part in the picture.

Something is **missing**!

Draw the missing part in the picture.

Something is **missing!**

Draw the missing part in the picture.

Something is **missing**!

Draw the missing part in the picture.

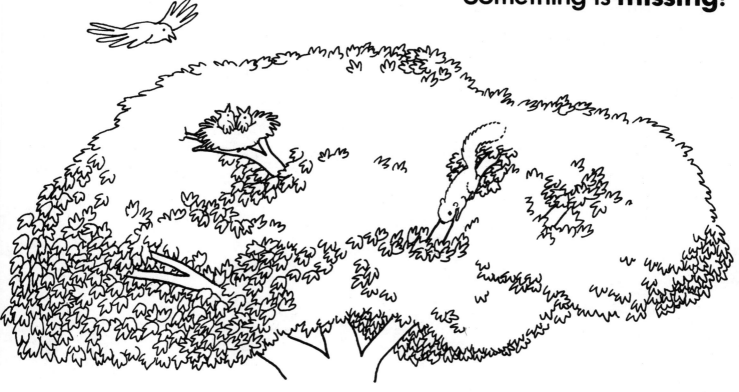

Draw the missing part in the picture.

Something is **missing!**

Draw the missing part in the picture.

Draw the missing part in the picture.

Something is **missing!**

Draw the missing part in the picture.

WRITE THE NUMBERS

0	**zero**	O
1 	**one**	
2	**two**	
3	**three**	
4	**four**	
5	**five**	

WRITE THE NUMBERS

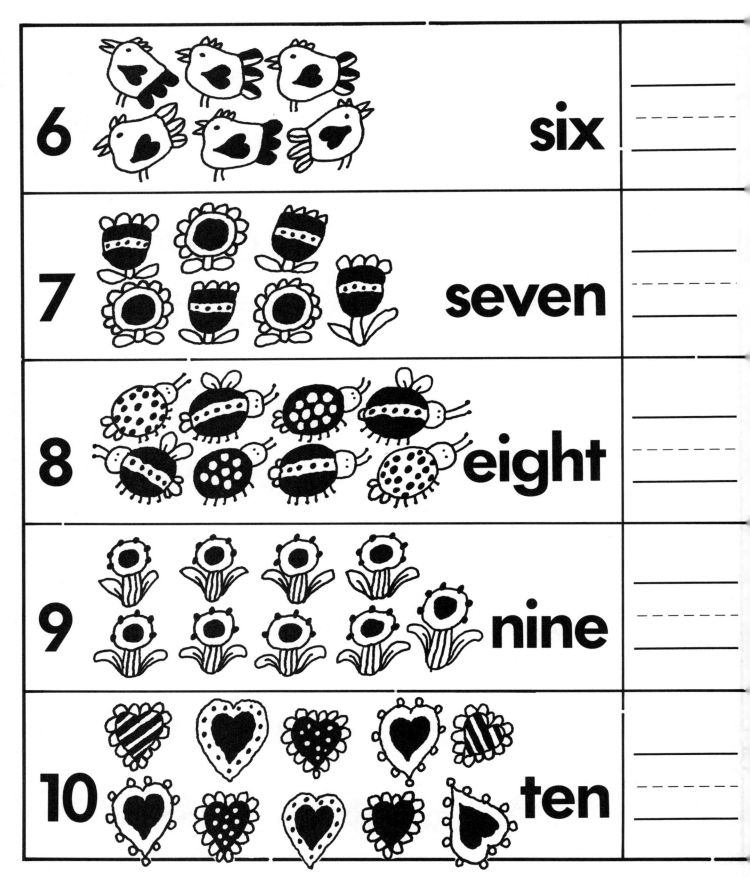

6   six   _____

7   seven   _____

8   eight   _____

9   nine   _____

10   ten   _____

FIND THE NUMBERS

The numbers 0, 1, 2, 3, 4, 5, 6, 7, 8, 9, and 10 are hidden in the picture.

Find the numbers and color them red.

COLOR THE PICTURE

1 = black 4 = blue 7 = purple

2 = red 5 = green 8 = brown

3 = yellow 6 = orange

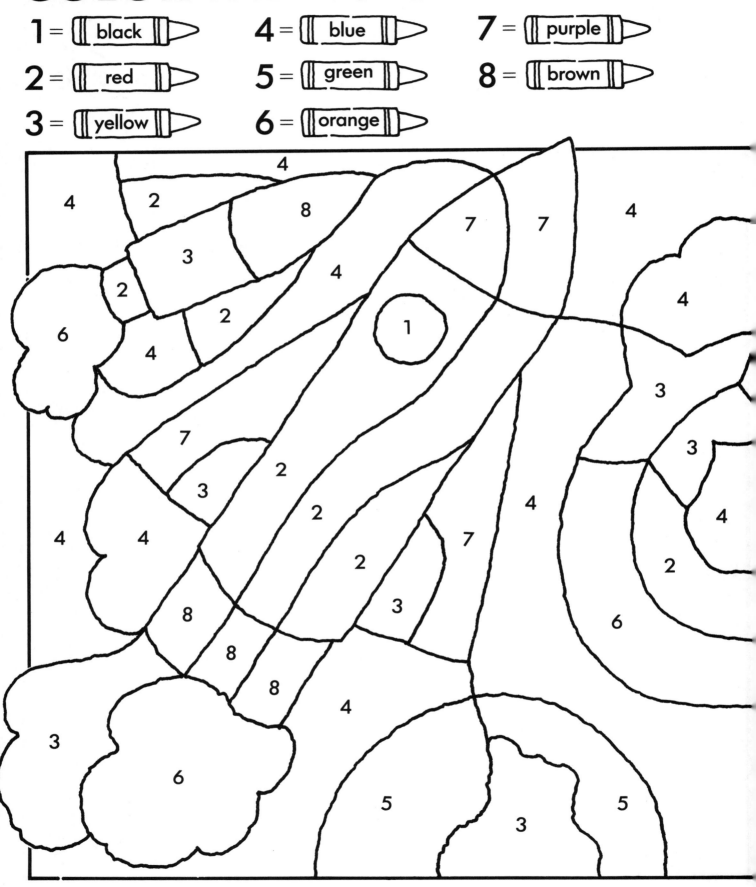

DOT-TO-DOT

Connect the dots. Begin with 0.

WRITE THE NUMBERS

11 eleven

12 twelve

13 thirteen

166

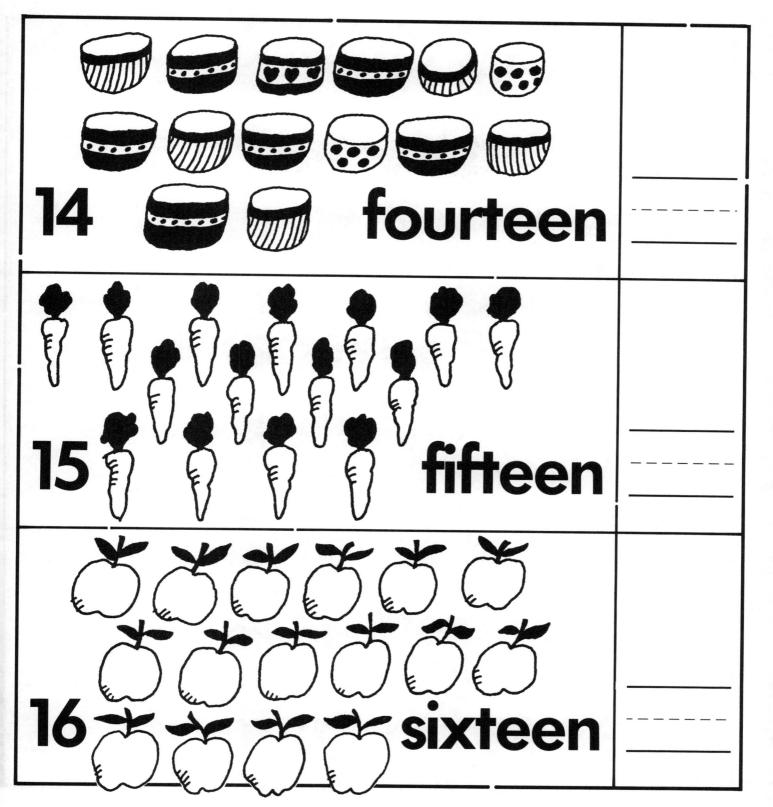

14 fourteen

15 fifteen

16 sixteen

WRITE THE NUMBERS

17 seventeen

18 eighteen

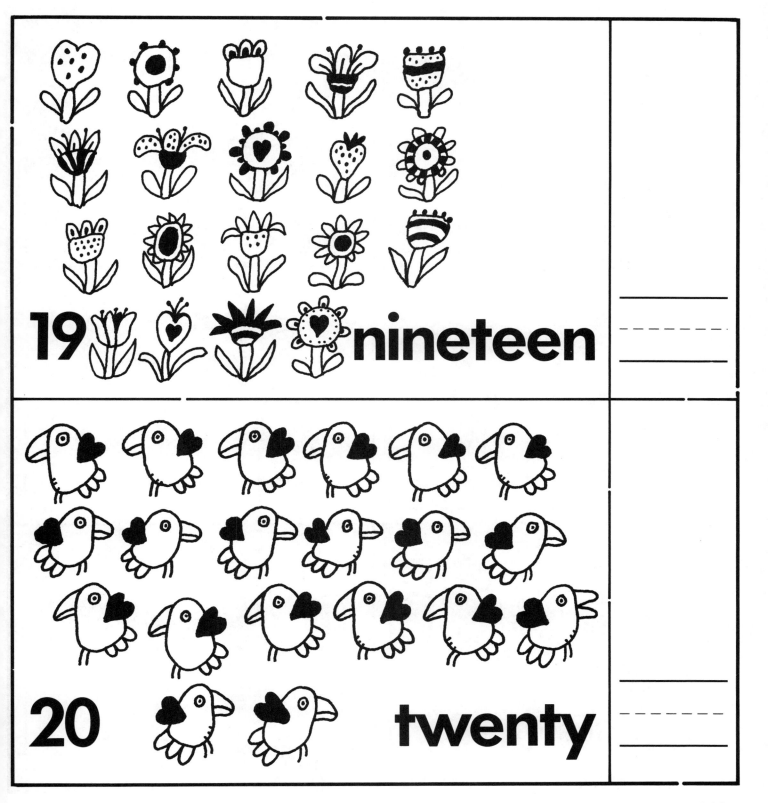

19 nineteen

20 twenty

HOW MANY?

How many things are there?
Count them.
Then write the number in the box.

DOT-TO-DOT

Connect the dots. Begin with 1.

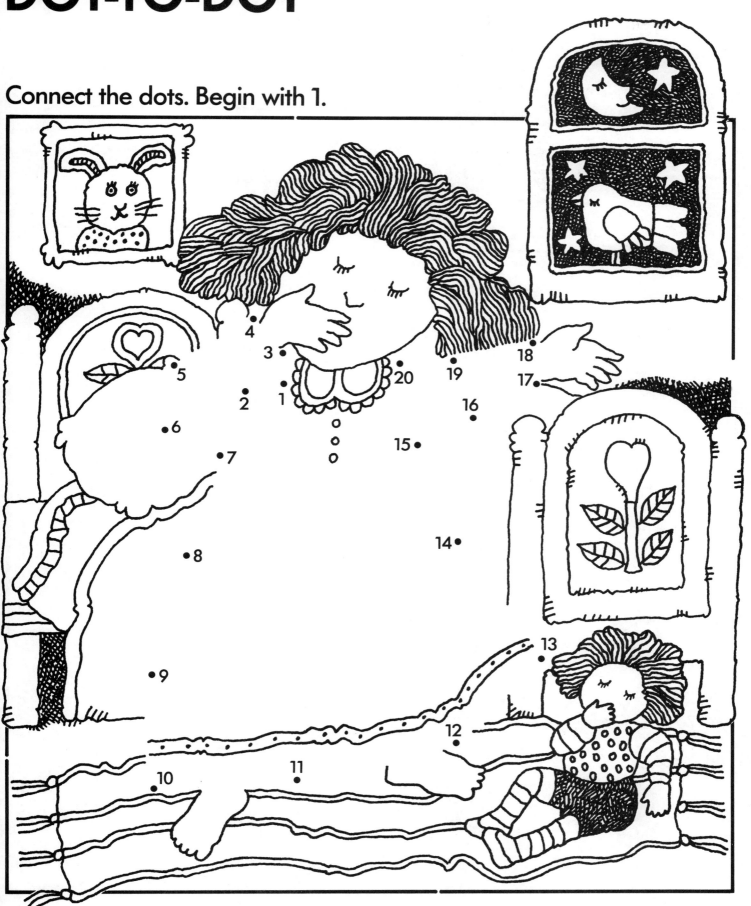

WHAT BELONGS BETWEEN?

The 5 belongs between the 4 and the 6.

4 5 6

Write the number that belongs between the other numbers.

7 ___ 9   2 ___ 4

9 ___ 11   1 ___ 3

8 ___ 10   5 ___ 7

WHAT COMES BEFORE?

The 6 comes before the 7.

_6_ **7 8**

Write the number that comes before the other numbers.

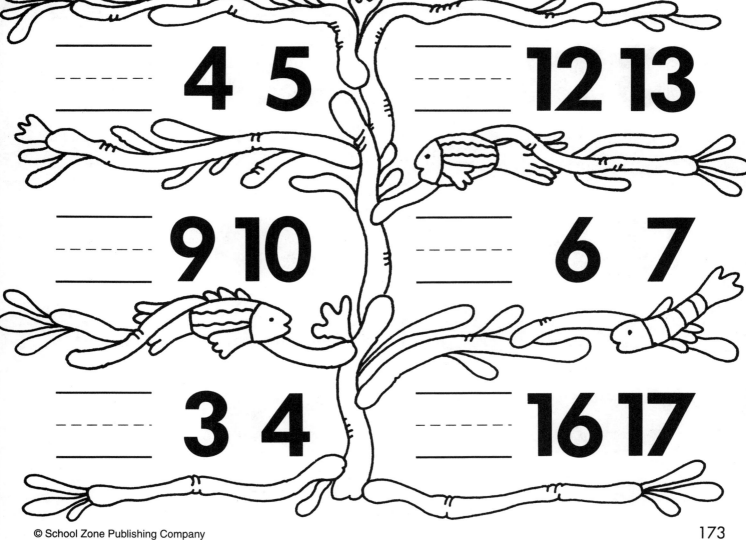

_____ **4 5**

_____ **12 13**

_____ **9 10**

_____ **6 7**

_____ **3 4**

_____ **16 17**

WHAT COMES AFTER?

The 7 comes after the 6.

5 6 7

Write the number that comes after the other numbers.

13 14 _____   3 4 _____

17 18 _____   8 9 _____

6 7 _____   10 11 _____

WHICH SET HAS FEWER?

Fewer means a smaller number of things.

Circle the set that has fewer things in it.

WHICH SET HAS FEWER?

Circle the number of the set that has fewer things in it.

Circle the set that is 2 fewer than the first set.

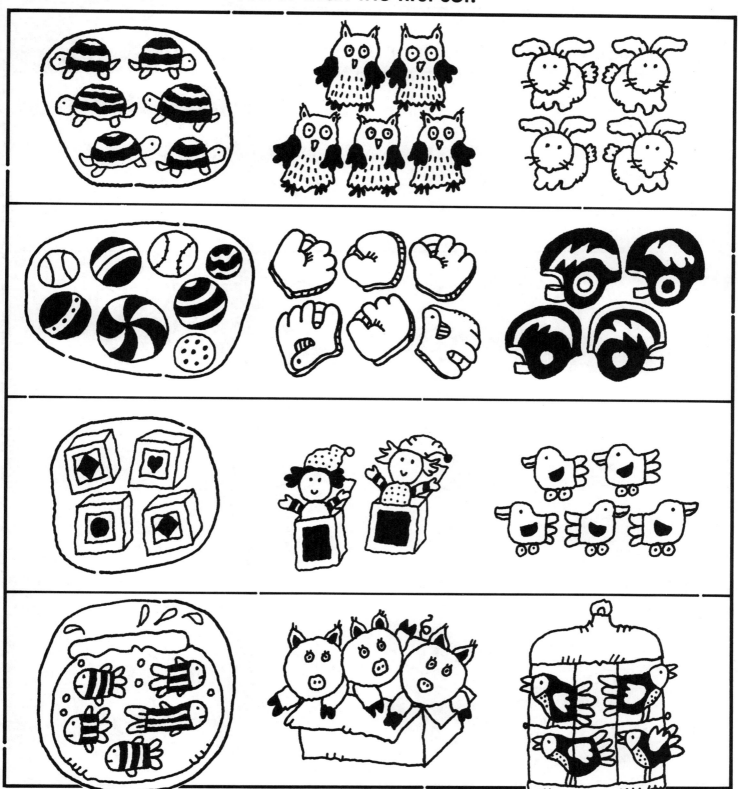

WHICH IS GREATER?

Greater means a bigger number of things.

Circle the set that has a greater number of things in it.

Circle the number of the set that has a greater number of things in it.

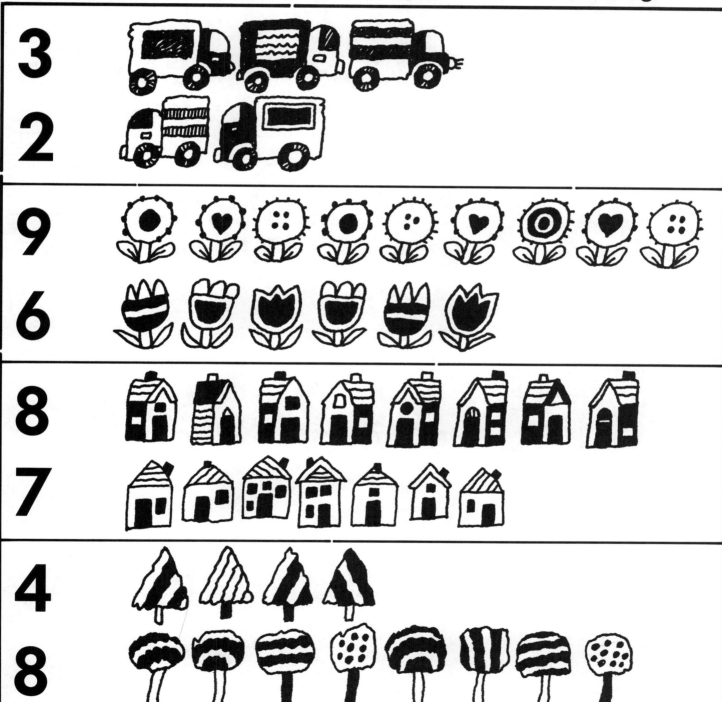

3
2

9
6

8
7

4
8

GREATER

Circle the set that is 3 greater than the first.

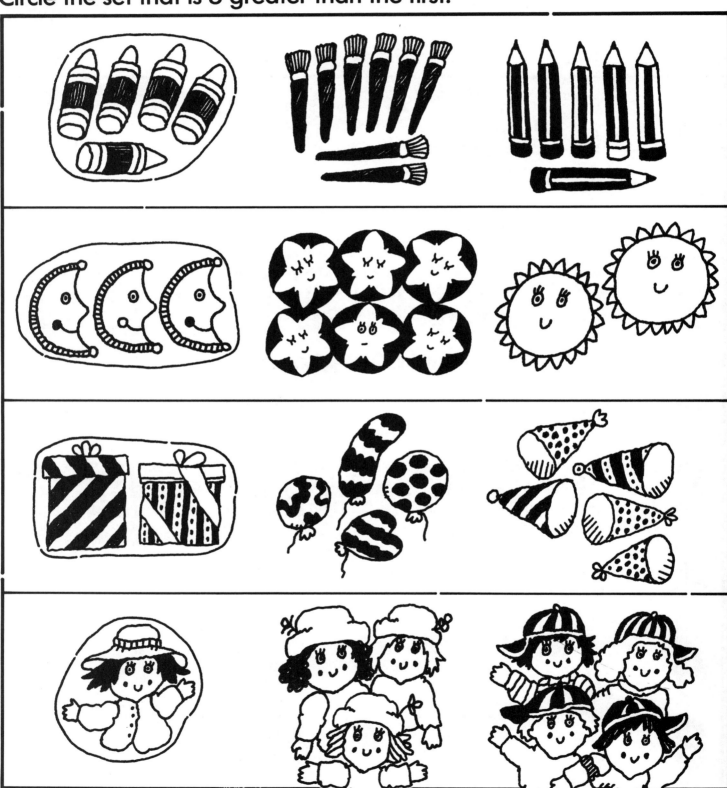

FIND THE NUMBERS

The numbers 5, 7, 8, 12, 13, 15, 16, 18, and 20 are hidden in the picture.

Find the numbers and color them blue.

SHAPES

Draw the shapes.

○
circle

△
triangle

□
square

▭
rectangle

182

○ △ □

Write the number 1 on each ○ .
Write the number 3 on each △ .
Write the number 4 on each □ .

TIME

A clock has two hands. The big hand points to the minutes. The little hand points to the hours.

Write the time.

3:00

_____
- - - - - - - - -
_____

_____
- - - - - - - - -
_____

_____
- - - - - - - - -
_____

Draw a line between the clocks that tell the same time.

TIME

Draw a small hand on each clock to show the correct time.

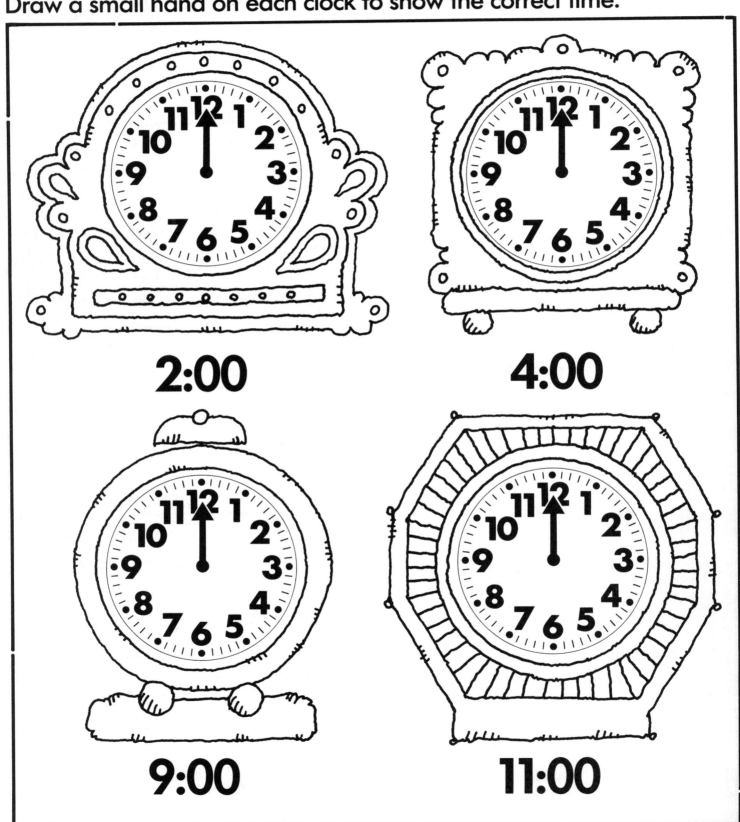

2:00

4:00

9:00

11:00

HIDDEN PICTURE

How many clocks say 4:00? _____

How many clocks say 9:00? _____

MONEY

Draw a line from each picture to the correct amount of money.

Write the amount of money that is inside each bank.

_____

_____

_____

_____

Circle what Jim can sell to make 24¢ today.

A Rhonda Rhinoceros Award

This is to certify that

name:

_____

- - - - - - - - - - - - - - - - - - - -

_____

**has completed the School Zone
TRANSITION MATH workbook.**

Rhonda Rhinoceros

I KNOW IT!

Circle the 2 pictures that begin with the **T** sound. ▬▬▬▬

TURTLE **T**

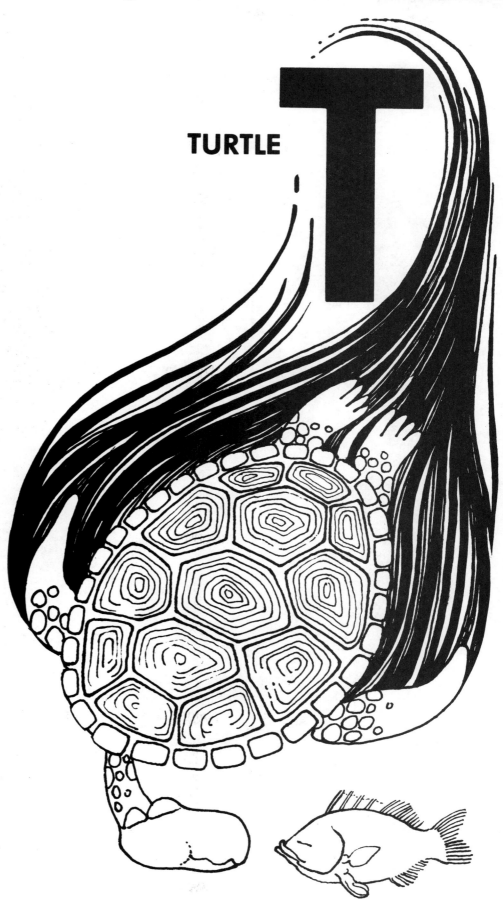

Circle the 2 pictures that begin with the M sound.

MONKEYS

194

Circle the 2 pictures that begin with the **B** sound. ▬▬▬

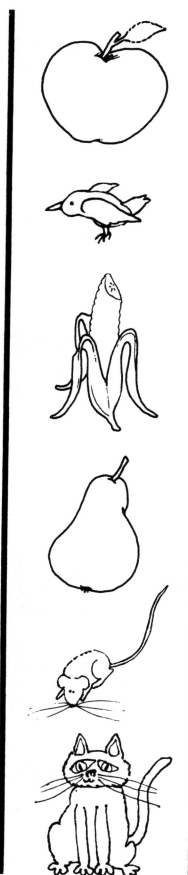

B

BICYCLE

Circle the 2 pictures that begin with the **S** sound.

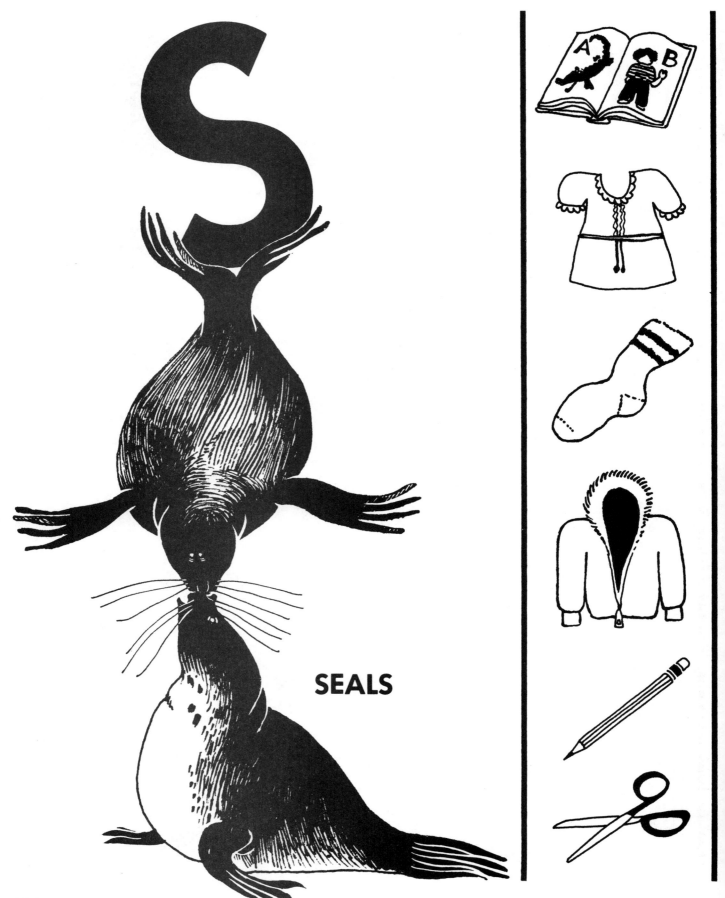

SEALS

Circle the 2 pictures that begin with the **P** sound. ▬▬▬▬

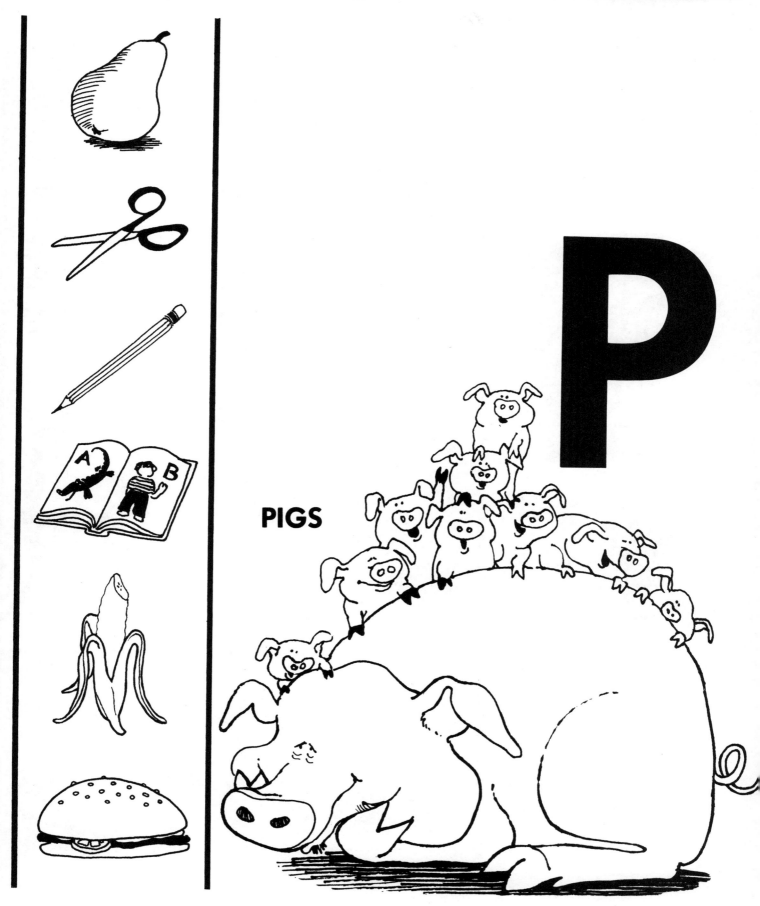

P

PIGS

FIND THE SAME SOUND

Circle the picture that begins with the same sound as the first one.

Circle the 2 pictures that begin with the **L** sound.

L

LEAVES

Circle the 2 pictures that begin with the N sound.

NUTS

Circle the 2 pictures that begin with the **D** sound. ▬▬▬▬▬

DOG

Circle the 2 pictures that begin with the **F** sound.

F
FOX

202

Circle the 2 pictures that begin with the **H** sound. ▬▬▬

HAT

FIND THE SAME SOUND

Circle the picture that begins with the same sound as the first one.

Circle the 2 pictures that begin with the **R** sound. ▬▬▬▬

ROOSTER

Circle the 2 pictures that begin with the **J** sound.

JEEP

Circle the 2 pictures that begin with the **K** sound. ▬▬▬▬

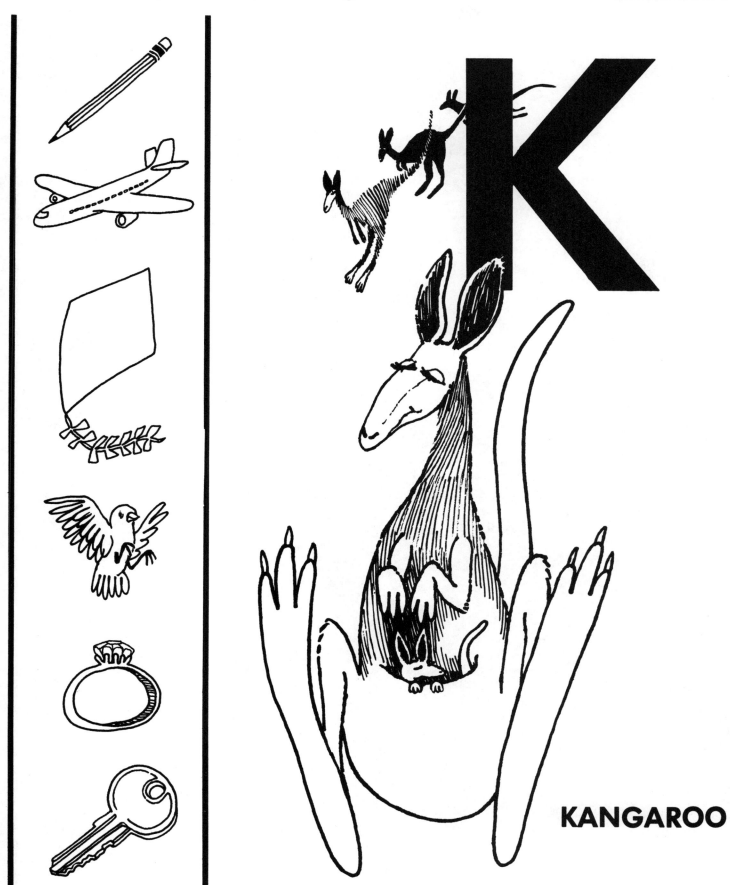

KANGAROO

Circle the 2 pictures that begin with the **W** sound.

WITCH

Circle the 2 pictures that begin with the **Y** sound. ▬▬▬▬

Y

YO-YOS

FIND THE SAME SOUND

Circle the picture that begins with the same sound as the first one.

Circle the 2 pictures that begin with the **V** sound. ▬▬▬

VALENTINES

Circle the 2 pictures that begin with the **Z** sound.

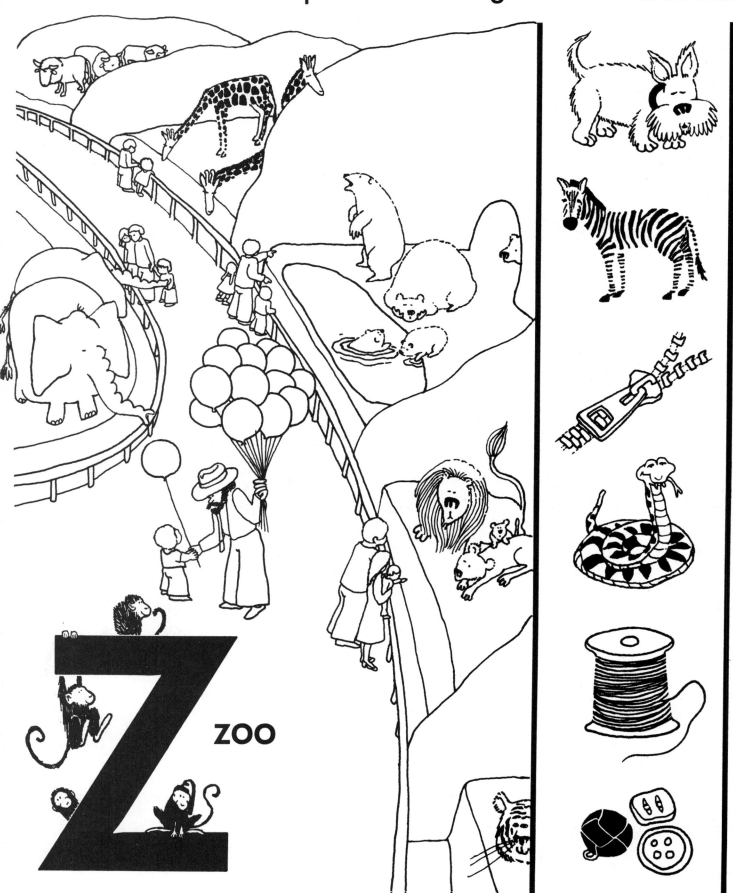

ZOO

Circle the 2 pictures that begin with the **Q** sound.

QUEEN

Circle the 2 pictures that begin with the **C** sound.

COW

Circle the 2 pictures that begin with the **G** sound. ▬▬

GATE

FIND THE
SAME
SOUND

Circle the picture that begins with the same sound as the first one.

Circle the 2 pictures that begin with the **A** sound.

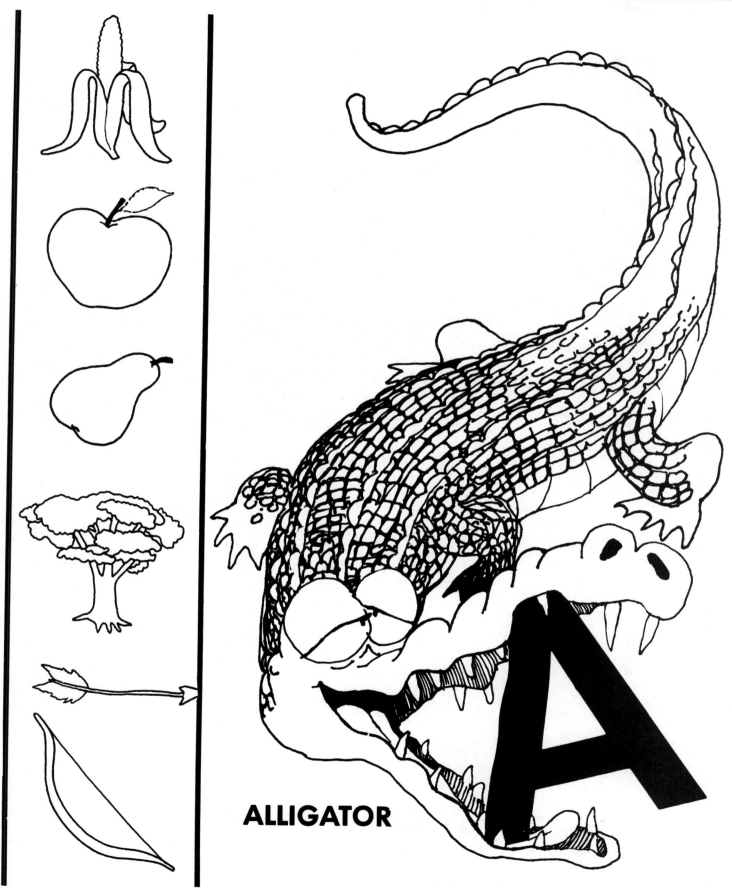

ALLIGATOR

Circle the 2 pictures that begin with the **E** sound.

E

ESKIMO

218

Circle the 2 pictures that begin with the **I** sound.

INK

Circle the 2 pictures that begin with the **O** sound.

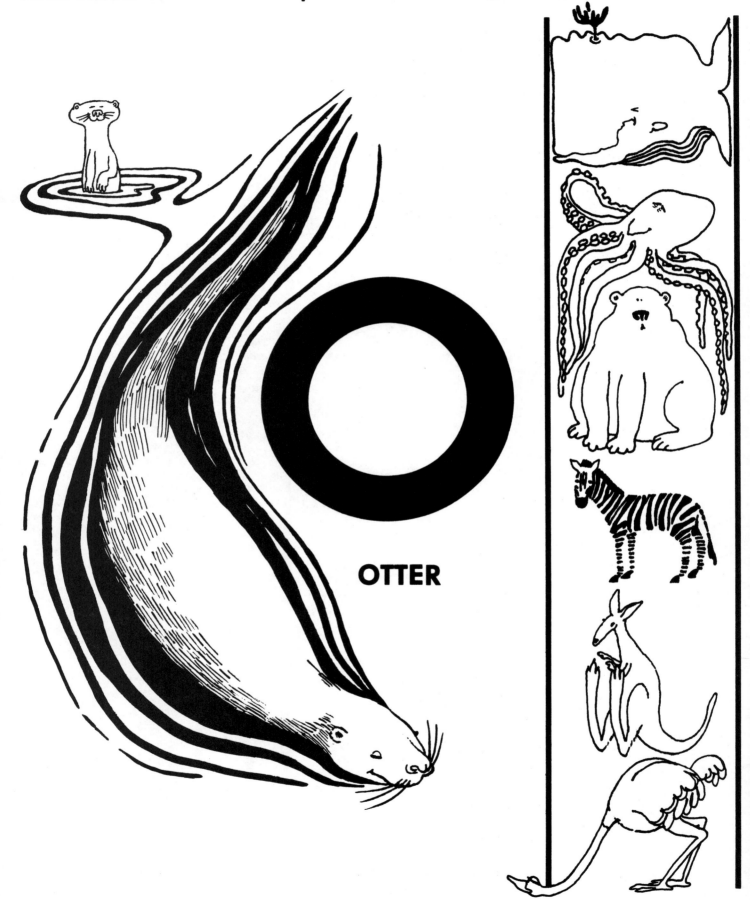

OTTER

Circle the 2 pictures that begin with the **U** sound. ▬▬▬

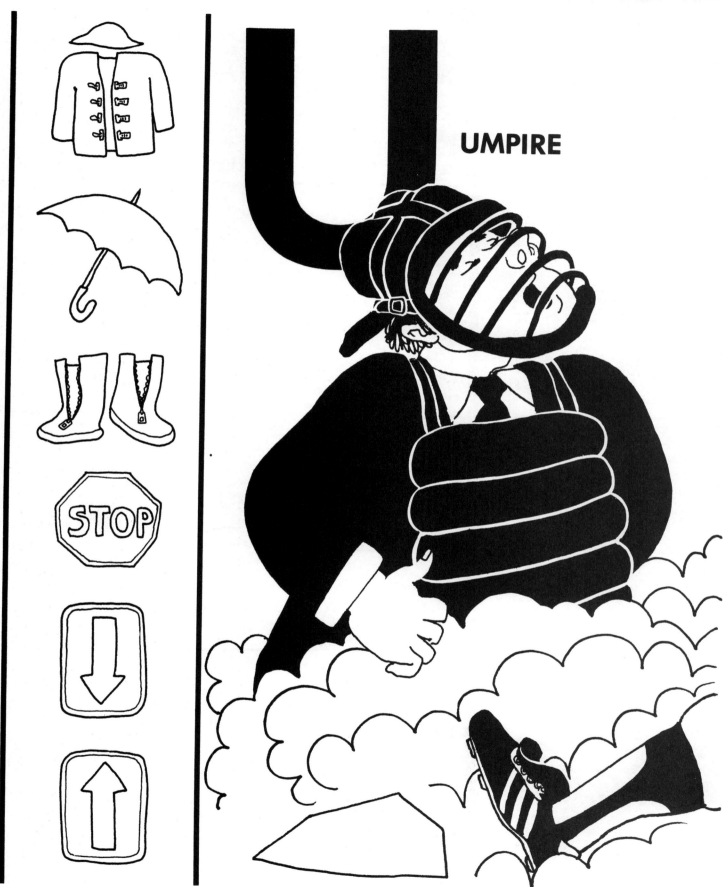

UMPIRE

FIND THE
SAME
SOUND

Circle the picture that begins with the same sound as the first one.

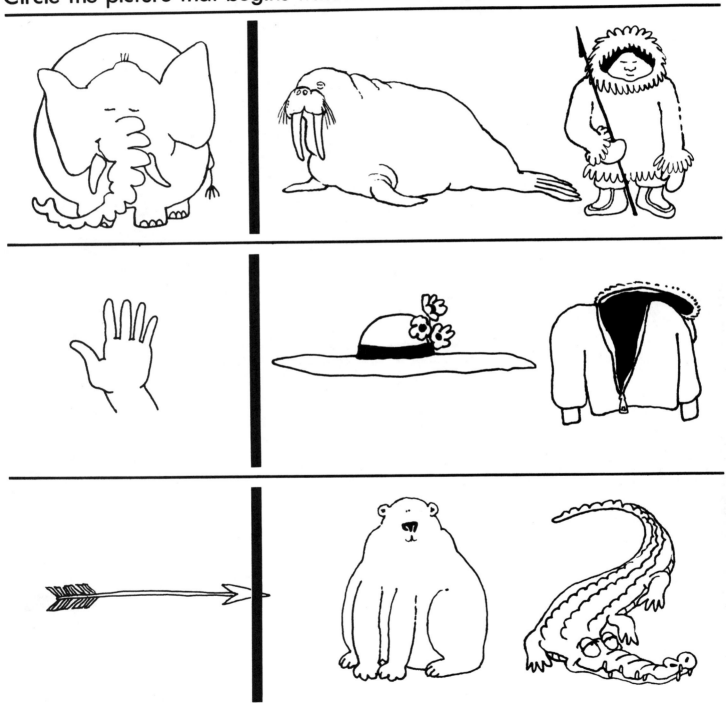

FIND THE RIGHT LETTER

Say the name of the picture.
Circle the letter that has the beginning sound of the picture.

   **B**   **V**

   **G**   **A**

   **L**   **A**

   **Z**   **M**

FIND THE RIGHT LETTER

Say the name of the picture.
Circle the letter that has the beginning sound of the picture.

R   B

T   F

A   I

U   Q

BIGGER

This  is big. This  is bigger.

Look at the pictures in each row.
Circle the picture that is bigger than the first picture.

SMALLER

This is small. This is smaller.

Look at the pictures in each row.
Circle the picture that is smaller than the first picture.

 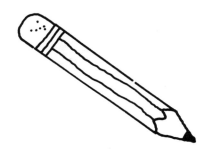  

SAME SIZE

These 🍎🍎 are the same size.

Look at the pictures in each box.
Circle the pictures that are the same size.

WHAT IS A SQUARE?

A square is a shape
that looks like this. □

Color each □ red.

WHAT IS A RECTANGLE?

A rectangle is a shape that looks like this. ☐

Circle the pictures that have a ☐ shape.

WHAT IS A CIRCLE?

A circle is a shape that looks like this. ○

Draw a line from the ○ to the things that have the same shape.

WHAT IS A TRIANGLE?

A triangle is a shape that looks like this. △

Color each △ yellow.

DIFFERENT

These are the same.

This is different.

Look at the pictures in each row.
Circle the picture that is different.

WHAT BELONGS?

A and  belong together.

Look at the pictures in each row.
Circle the picture that belongs with the first picture.

      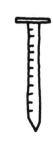   

Draw a line from the to the things that belong with it.

WHAT BELONGS?

A  belongs in a 🏠.

Draw a line from the 🏠 to what belongs in it.

Where do the animals belong?
Draw a line from each animal to its house.

MAKE A PAIR

A  and make a pair.

A and do not make a pair.

Look at the pictures in each row.
Circle the two pictures that make a pair.

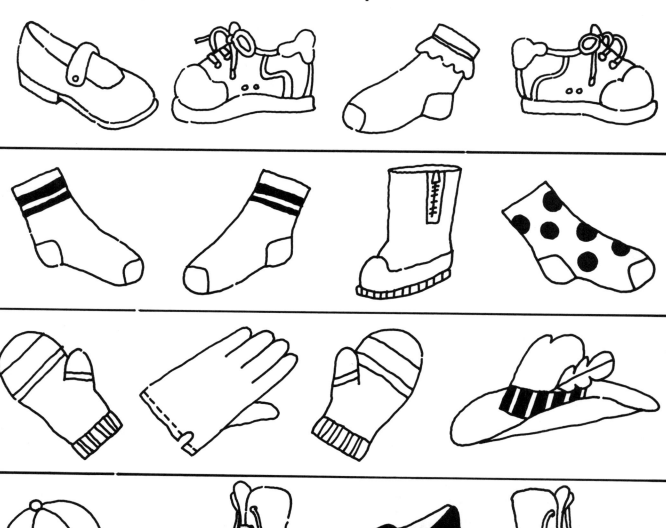

A 🧤 and 🧤 make a pair.

A 🧤 and 🧤 do not make a pair.

Look at the pictures in each row.
Circle the two pictures that make a pair.

WHAT IS MISSING?

Look at the pictures.
Then look at the missing parts.
Draw in each where it belongs.

OPPOSITES

This 🤡 is happy.

This 🤡 is sad.

Happy is the opposite of sad.

Draw a line from each word to the picture of its opposite.

dirty

night

up

242

Circle the picture that shows the opposite of the first picture.

soft

full

hot

RHYMING

  rhymes with .

Look at the pictures in each box.
Circle the two pictures whose words rhyme.

Look at the picture below.

The  is a hen.

Draw a line from the to the pictures

whose words rhyme with hen.

FEWER

Fewer means a smaller number of things.

Look at the pictures in each row.
Circle the set that has fewer things in it.

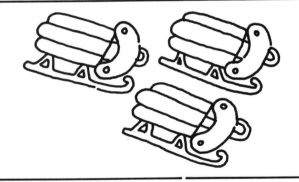

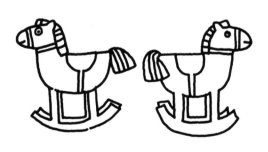

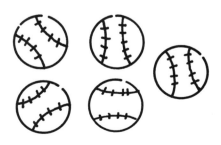

GREATER

Greater means a bigger number of things.

Look at the pictures in each row.
Circle the set that has a greater number of things in it.

FIRST, NEXT, LAST

Write 1 in the circle to show what happened first.
Write 2 to show what happened next.
Write 3 to show what happened last.

248

FIRST, NEXT, LAST

Write 1 in the circle to show what happened first.
Write 2 to show what happened next.
Write 3 to show what happened last.

BEFORE

A comes before B.

Write the letter that comes before the other letter.

ABCDEFGHIJKL
MNOPQRSTUVWXYZ

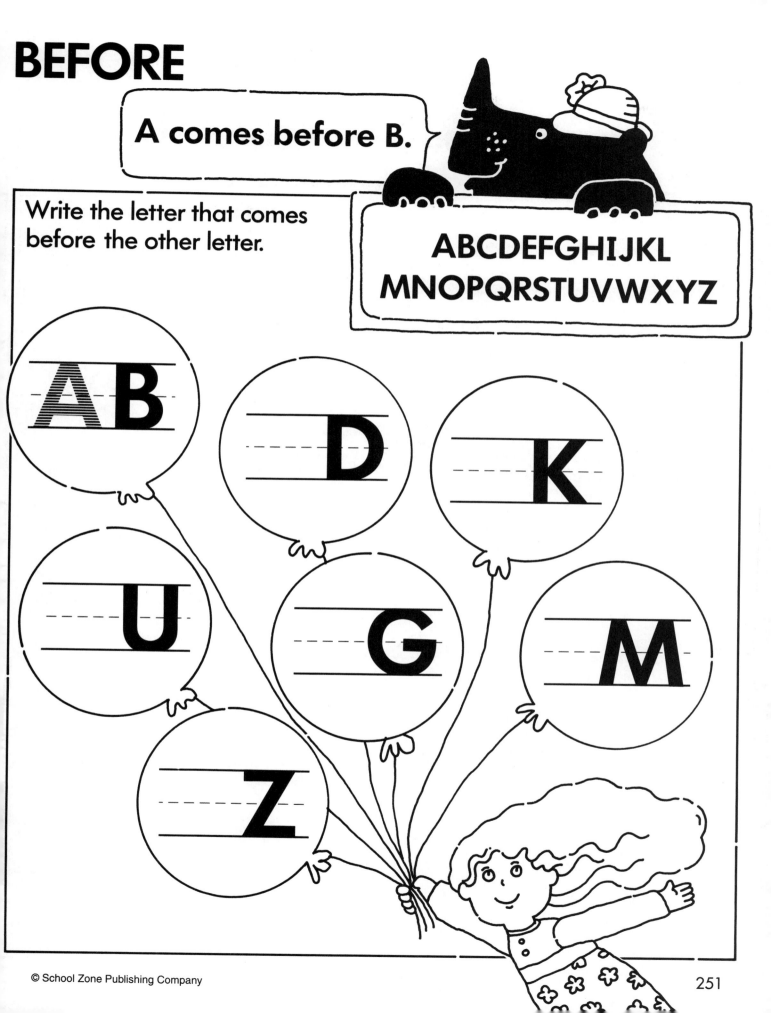

BETWEEN

B comes between A and C.

ABCDEFGHIJKL
MNOPQRSTUVWXYZ

Write the letter that comes between the other letters.

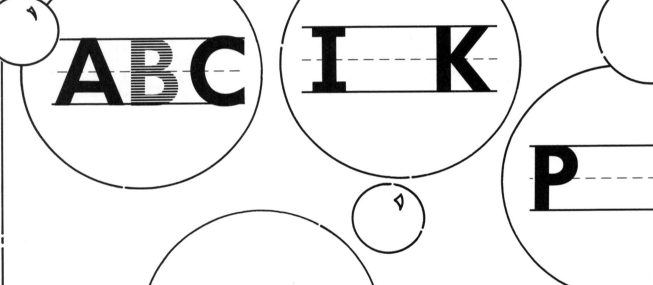

A B C

I K

P R

H J

T V

AFTER

C comes after B.

ABCDEFGHIJKL
MNOPQRSTUVWXYZ

Write the letter that comes after the other letter.

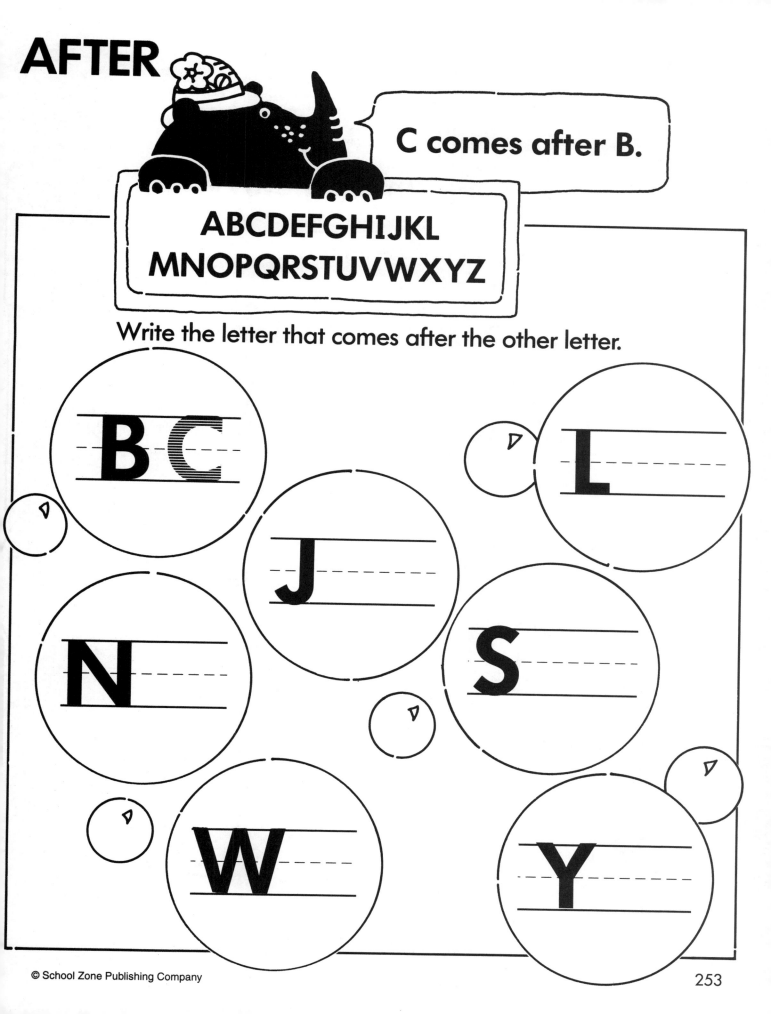

LETTER MATCH

abcdefghijkl
mnopqrstuvwxyz

Draw a line from each upper-case letter
to the correct lower-case letter.

254

Write the correct lower-case letter next to each upper-case letter.

A Rhonda Rhinoceros
Award

This is to certify that

name:

_____

- -

_____

**has completed the School Zone
READING READINESS 1 workbook.**

Rhonda Rhinoceros

I KNOW IT!

256

FILL IN THE LETTERS

Fill in each blank with the letter that comes next.

A   _____   _____   D   _____

_____   _____   H   _____   _____

_____   L   _____   _____   _____

P   _____   _____   _____   T   _____

_____   _____   X   _____   Z

LETTER MATCH

Draw a line from each uppercase letter to its lowercase letter.

WHAT ORDER?

Write each set of letters in the correct order.

F E D

P O Q

T S R

M L N

BEGINNING SOUNDS

Say each picture word.
Write its first letter.
Then write the word on the line.

__op

__ent

__est

__ut

260

m p

__oon

_____
- - - - - - - - - - -
_____

__ig

_____
- - - - - - - - - - -
_____

__an

_____
- - - - - - - - - - -
_____

__an

_____
- - - - - - - - - - -
_____

ENDING SOUNDS

Say each picture word.
Write its last letter.
Then write the word on the line.

d   t
___ ___

be___

_____
- - - - - - - - - -
_____

goa___

_____
- - - - - - - - - -
_____

ca___

_____
- - - - - - - - - -
_____

han___

_____
- - - - - - - - - -
_____

m n

su__

_____

- - - - - - - - - -

_____

gu__

_____

- - - - - - - - - -

_____

dru__

_____

- - - - - - - - - -

_____

fa__

_____

- - - - - - - - - -

_____

FIRST, NEXT, LAST

Write 1 in the circle to show what happened first.
Write 2 to show what happened next.
Write 3 to show what happened last.

WHICH TWO GO TOGETHER?

Draw a line from each little picture to the correct big picture.

Circle the words of the two things that go together.

hat   bone   dog

shoe   sock   bird

bee   car   flower

bucket   ball   mop

ONE DOES NOT BELONG

Circle the word of the thing that does not belong.

hand

tree

foot   box

horn   drum

bed

fork

pillow   fan

spoon   fox

goat

ring

pig

house

fish

barn

bird

apple

orange

coat

cow

hat

NUMBER WORDS

Color two 🧸 yellow.

Color four 🎈 blue.

Color three 🎀 red.

Color one 🐊 green.

270

Circle the set of 7.
Draw a square around the set of 6.

ten

seven

nine

six

eight

COLOR THE PICTURE

Color the  green.

Color the 🌞 yellow.

Color the blue.

Color the purple.

Color the orange.

Color the brown.

Color the red.

Color the black.

Color the white.

272

© School Zone Publishing Company

WORDS THAT RHYME

Circle the words that rhyme with **sing**.
Draw a square around the words that rhyme with **ran**.

fan

ring

man

pan

king

can

swing

Circle the words that rhyme with **rat**.
Draw a square around the words that rhyme with **lake**.

snake

bat

cat

mat

rake

cake

hat

WHICH IS IT?

Write the names of the animals on the left.
Write the names of the plants on the right.

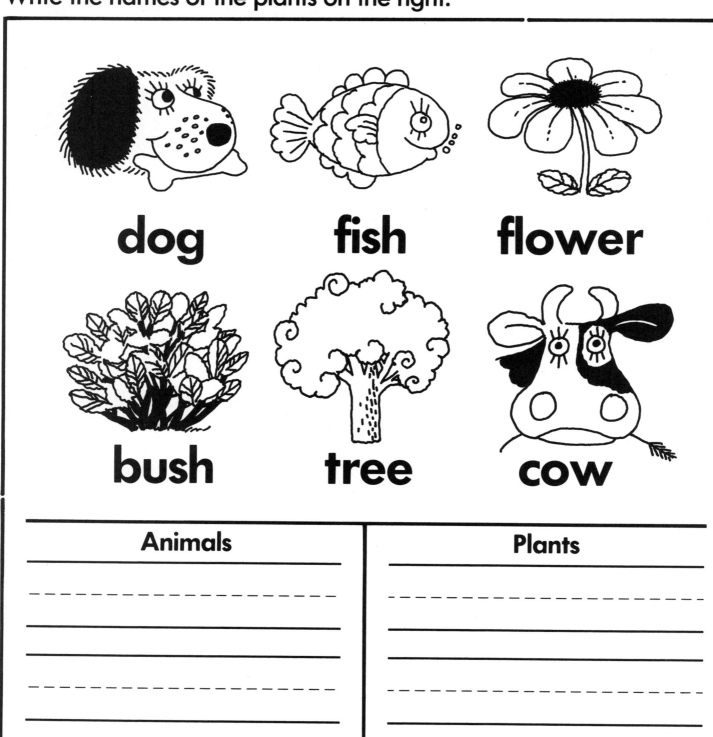

dog   fish   flower

bush   tree   cow

Animals	Plants

Draw a line from the foods to the .
Draw a line from the toys to the .

apple

berry

doll

jacks

ball

cake

WORDS

Draw a line from each word to the correct picture.

man

jam

pan

ham

fan

278

Draw a line from each picture to the correct word.

hen

goat

men

boat

pen

WHERE IS IT?

over   by   under   in

Write the correct word to tell where the bird is.

The bird is _____ the  .

The bird is _____ the  .

Write the correct word to tell where the bird is.

The bird is _____ **the**  **.**

The bird is _____ **the**  **.**

WHERE IS IT?

on   **by**   **under**

Draw a red 🍎 under the ⌁ .

Draw a green 🍎 on the ⌁ .

Draw a yellow 🍎 by the ⌁ .

IN, ON, AND UNDER

Write the correct number on each line.

How many 🐕 are under the 🪑 ? _____

How many 🐟 are in the 🏺 ? _____

How many 🐱 are on the 🪑 ? _____

ALPHABETICAL ORDER

Write the words in a-b-c order.

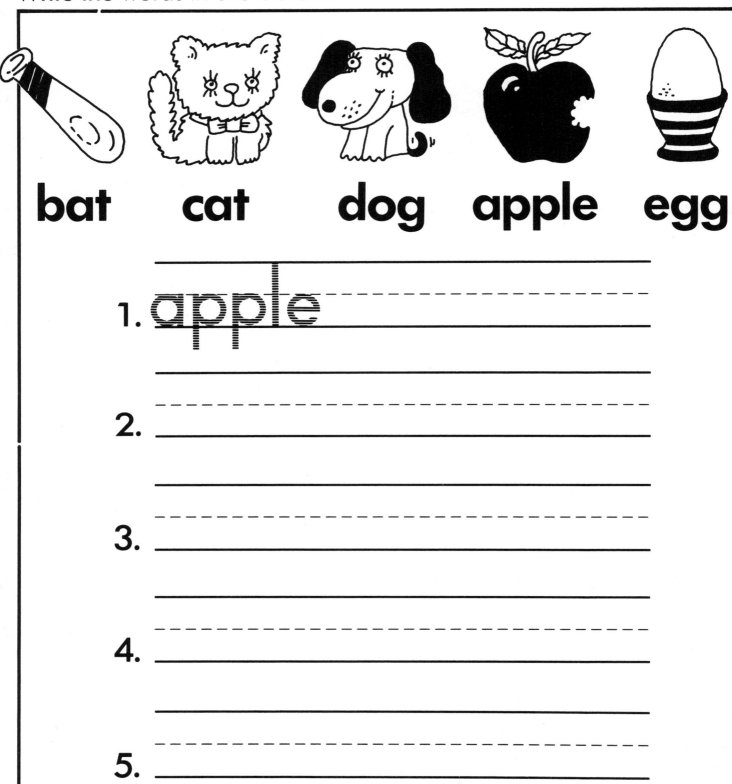

bat　　cat　　dog　　apple　　egg

1. apple

2.

3.

4.

5.

ABCDEFGHIJKLMNOPQRSTUVWXYZ

Write the words in a-b-c order.

goat   duck   fox   car   elf

1. car

2.

3.

4.

5.

ABCDEFGHIJKLMNOPQRSTUVWXYZ

WHAT DO YOU SEE?

Underline the sentence that goes with each picture.

See the ball.

See the dog.

See the boat.

See the dog.

See the boat.

See the ball.

See the doll.

See the boat.

Underline the sentences that tell what you see.

There are two cows.

There are four balls.

There is a house.

There is one goat.

There is a girl.

A Rhonda Rhinoceros Award

This is to certify that

name:

_____

- -

_____

**has completed the School Zone
READING READINESS 2 workbook.**

Rhonda Rhinoceros

I KNOW IT!

288

Circle the part that is **missing** in the picture.

Then draw the **missing** part in the picture.

Circle the part that is **missing** in the picture.

Then draw the **missing** part in the picture.

Circle the part that is **missing** in the picture.

Then draw the **missing** part in the picture.

Circle the part that is **missing** in the picture.

Then draw the **missing** part in the picture.

Circle the **hidden** , the , and the .

Circle the **hidden** ♡, 🐯, and 〰️.

Circle the letter **A**. Circle the letter **C**. Circle the letter **K**.

Color the **2** 🚗 .

Circle the **2** that are the **same**.

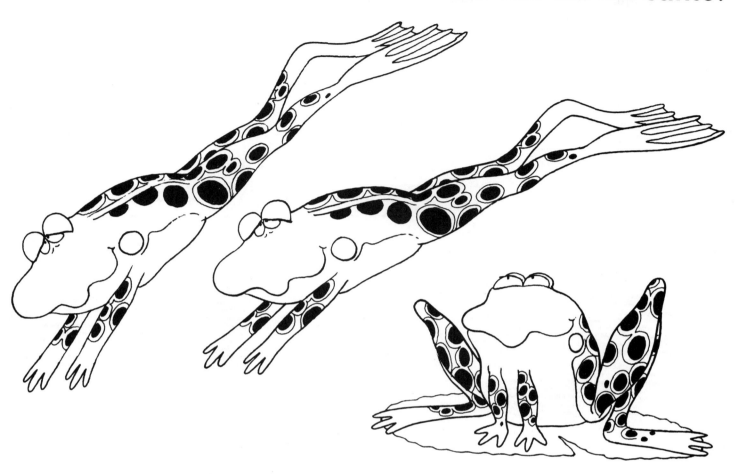

Circle the **2** that are the **same** in each group.

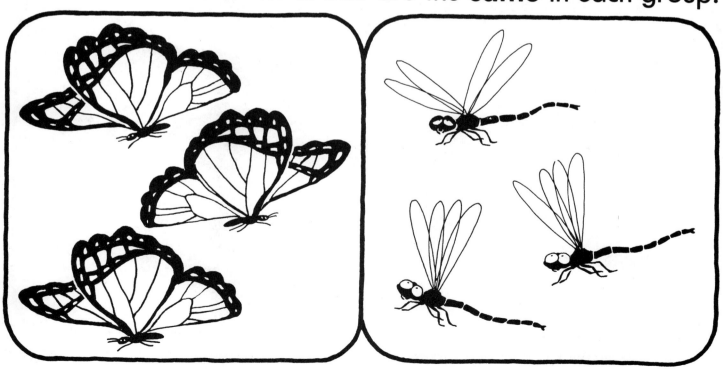

Circle the **2** that are the **same**.

Circle the **2** that are the **same** in each group.

Circle the **2** that are the **same**.

Circle the **2** that are the **same** in each group.

Circle the **2** that are the **same**.

Circle the **2** that are the **same** in each group.

Circle the picture that **rhymes** with the big one.

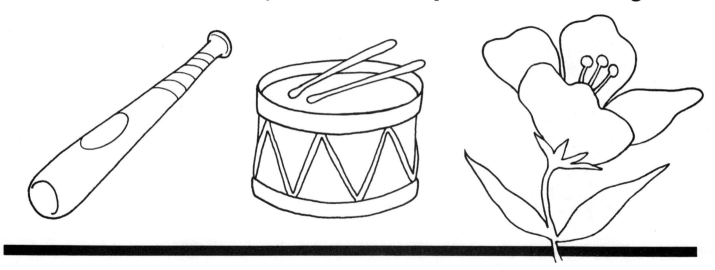

Circle the picture that **rhymes** with the big one.

Circle the picture that **rhymes** with the big one.

Circle the picture that **rhymes** with the big one.

304

Help the boy find his shoe.

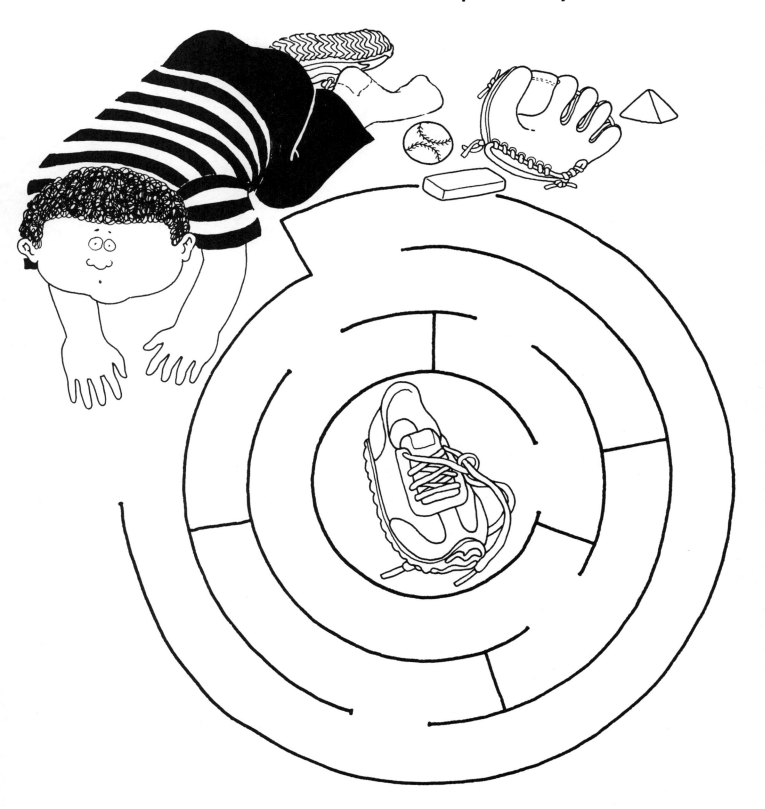

Draw a line that shows how he must go.

Help the mouse get to the cheese.

Draw a line that shows how she must go.

Help the bear go for a swim.

Draw a line that shows how he must go.

Help the divers find the treasure.

Draw a line that shows how they must go.

Connect the dots from **1** to **10** to finish the picture.

Connect the dots from **1** to **10** to finish the picture.

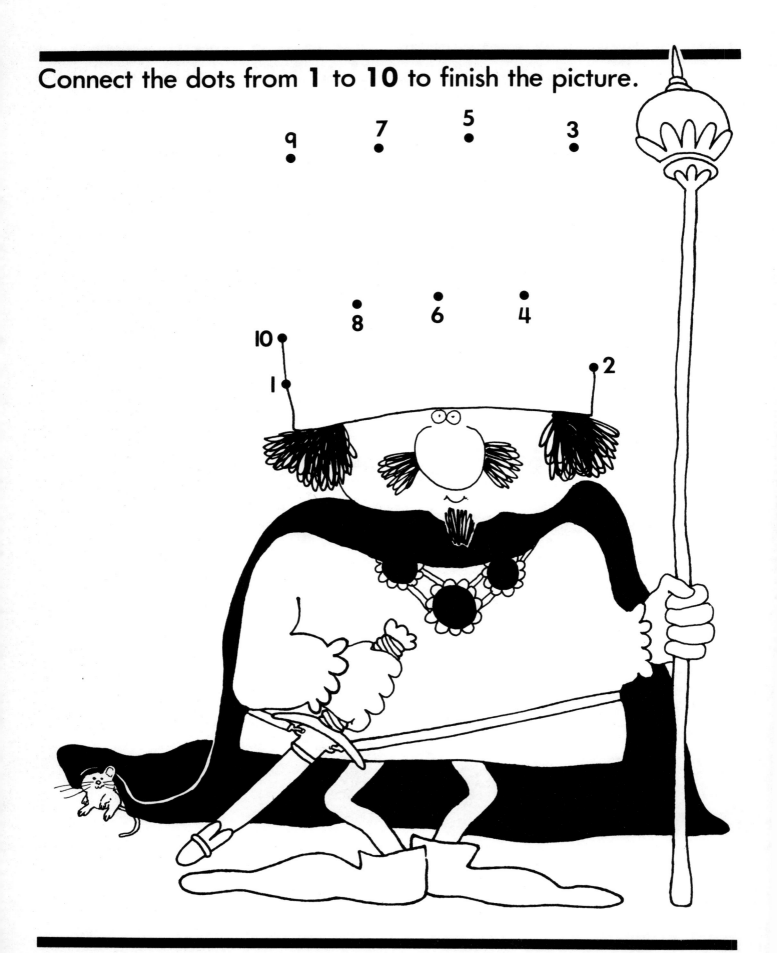

Connect the dots from **1** to **10** to finish the picture.

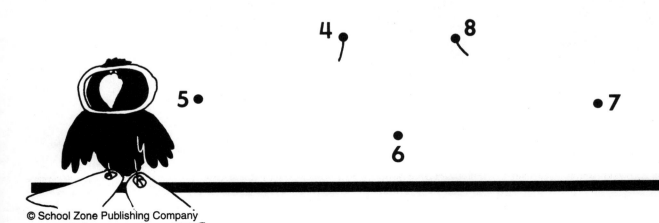

Connect the dots from **1** to **10** to finish the picture.

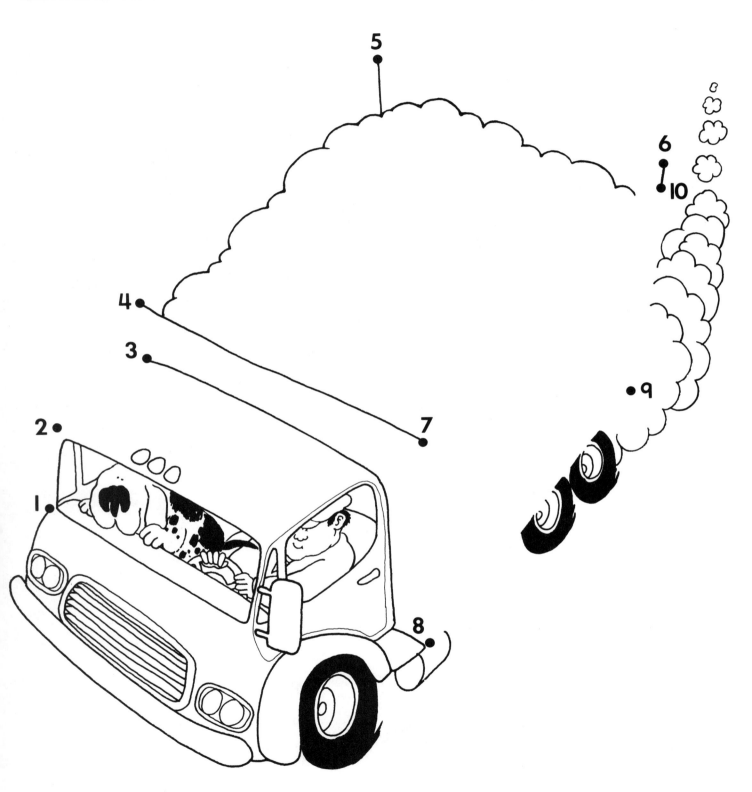

Circle the picture that **belongs** with the first one.

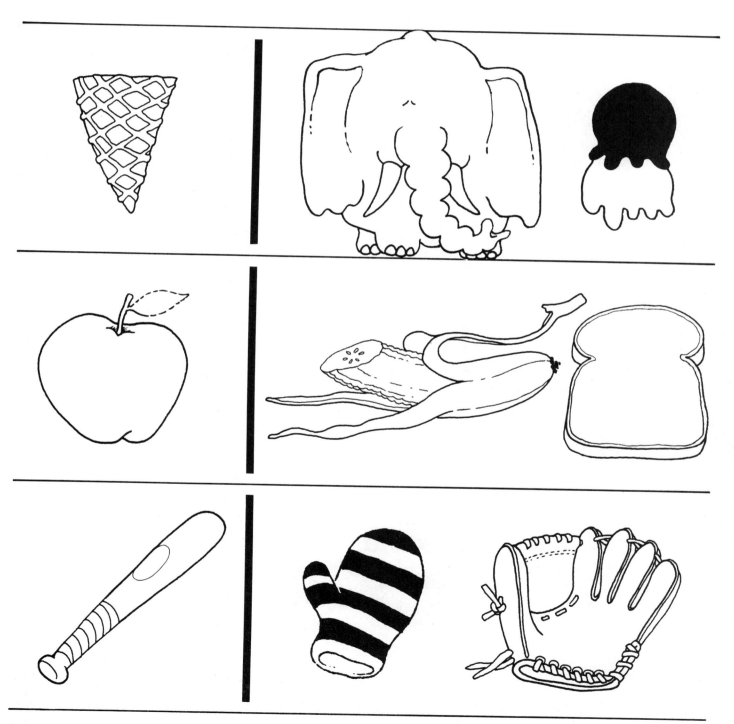

Circle the picture that **belongs** with the first one.

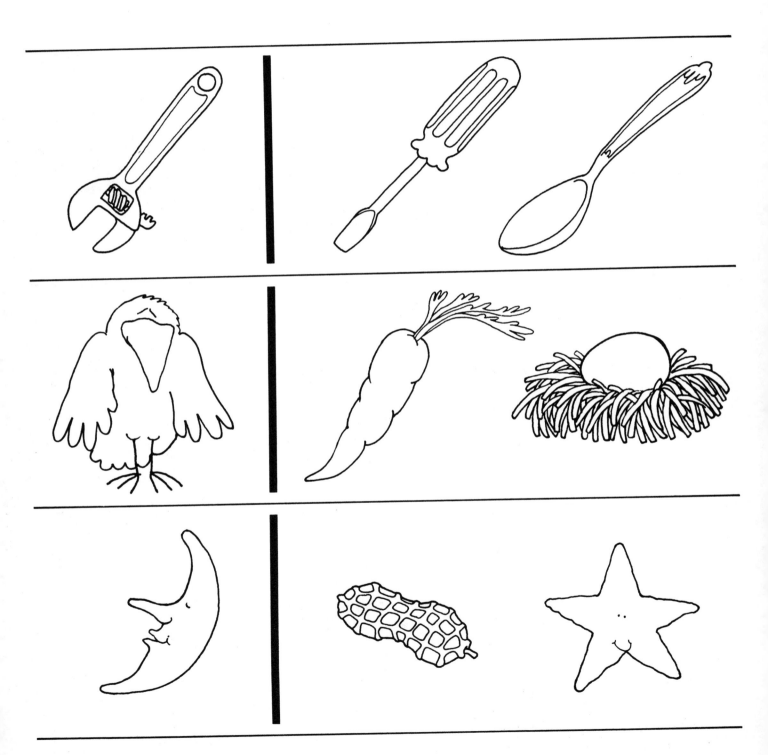

Circle the picture that **belongs** with the first one.

Circle the picture that **belongs** with the first one.

Circle the **3** ▢ shapes.

Circle the **3** ◯ shapes.

Circle the **3** ▬ shapes.

Circle the **3** ▲ shapes.